SECRET NEW YORK CITY

A Guide to the Weird, Wonderful, and Obscure

Rossilynne Skena Culgan

Reedy Press
PO Box 5131
St. Louis, MO 63139
reedypress.com

Library of Congress Control Number: 2024939252
ISBN: 9781681065601

Design by Jill Halpin

Unless otherwise indicated, all cover and interior photos are courtesy of the author or believed to be in the public domain. Mural art, bottom left on the front cover, is courtesy of Leonard Zhukovsky/Shutterstock.

Printed in the United States of America
24 25 26 27 28   5 4 3 2 1

To those who are willing to take the scenic route

There are secrets to be found everywhere in New York City—even at the busiest, unlikeliest places.

CONTENTS

New York City isn't all bright lights and honking horns. Instead, quiet oases can be found across the five boroughs—you just need to know where to look.

ACKNOWLEDGMENTS

Frank Sinatra crooned about the ability to "make it" here, and I don't know exactly what that means for a New Yorker in this era. But to me, writing this book feels as close as I've gotten so far. It was an honor to research and write these vignettes about New York City, the best city in the world. I'd be remiss, however, if I also didn't acknowledge the significant challenges of this project and the people who buoyed me through it.

Thank you to everyone who spilled their New York secrets. I am in awe of, and grateful to, the artists, historians, and guardians of these places that make this city so special (and so wonderfully weird). To everyone who allowed me to interview you, answered my many questions, and shared photos: this book would not have been possible without you.

Thank you to my Time Out New York colleagues and friends—especially Delia Barth, Mykal Bayne, Will Gleason, Onik Hossain, Sarah Iandoli, Gloria Kim, Ian Kumamoto, Anna Rahmanan, and Shaye Weaver—who supplied ideas, edits, and endless encouragement. My "research assistants," aka dear friends Katie Johnston and Heather Schmelzlen, made my long research treks a lot of fun. My BFF Michelle Terek supported me from afar, along with Grace Muller, Megan Zhang, Lexi Belculfine, Leslie Stahl, Tanika D'Souza, and Prakruti Bhatt whose enthusiasm spanned the miles. Wise professors David Hajdu and Alisa Solomon helped me think deeply about NYC's arts and culture. My "writing assistant," Cleocatra, reminded me to rest and inspired me to donate a portion of every book sold to local animal charities.

Thank you to the entire team at Reedy Press and to fellow authors Jessica Mlinaric and Jonah McDonald, who invited me into their "Secret" club.

I could shout "thank you" from atop the Empire State Building until I was hoarse, and it would never be enough to adequately thank my lifelines. Mom and Dad, thank you for always reading every word.

Finally, to Shane, my partner in every adventure, including making a life together in New York City: every paragraph is better because of your edits, and every day is better because of your love.

Art is around every corner here, from sound art to sculptures to this graffiti wall in East Harlem.

INTRODUCTION

New York City is a hard place to keep a secret. With 8.4 million people, including more than a million packed onto the dense island of Manhattan, it's tough to leave much to the imagination.

But after walking hundreds of miles across the five boroughs, spending hours on subway trains, talking to lots of locals, scouring old newspapers, and reading to the end of the internet, I've discovered some of the city's lesser-known spots. Some are secrets hiding in plain sight—the kind of thing you might walk past every day and never notice. Others are tucked away, and you have to know where to go find them.

It turns out there are secrets everywhere in this busy city: inside Civil War ruins, at subway stations, and within places that reveal the revolutionary history of America. The more I researched, the more I found myself noticing camouflaged details—a subtle change in flooring inside the Oculus, an often-ignored plaque inside Macy's, or a street sign that looks a little unusual in Queens.

Despite featuring dozens of secrets, this book only scratches the surface of the weird, wonderful, and obscure nooks and crannies of New York City. Consider these items, presented in random order across all five boroughs, as a treasure map. As an added bonus, many are free to visit, a rarity in New York City.

Whether you're a New York City native, someone who fulfilled their dream of moving here (as I did), or a visitor, I hope these stories will encourage you to go out and explore all this city has to offer—not just the places that get attention in the typical guidebooks. You're in the right place to start that journey because this book is anything but ordinary. So lace up your sneakers, and let's get out there.

ART WITHIN REACH

What's that green metal thing in the 34th Street-Herald Square subway station?

Inside the 34th Street-Herald Square subway station, a green metal box hangs above the uptown and downtown N/R train platforms. Several vents, some small rectangular holes, and clear crystal-shaped pieces dot this strange piece of metal. It looks like ductwork or perhaps some kind of wiring channel. Quite simply, it's not much to look at.

But the curious straphanger who is willing to reach their hand in front of the holes will be met with pure magic. A simple wave activates this delightful piece of public artwork, which plays musical instruments like the marimba and flute, as well as environmental sounds such as what you might hear in the Everglades or the rainforest. Suddenly, amid the station announcements and the clanging trains, the station fills with songs of birds, tree frogs, and musical notes. Those crystal-shaped pieces light up, adding spectacular illumination to the show.

As soon as one brave soul starts playing with the artwork, more will invariably follow. Even better, because the instruments are positioned on both the uptown and downtown lines, people across the tracks can play together. It's joyful enough to wring a smile out of even the surliest transit-goer.

The artwork, called *REACH*, was designed by artist-composer Christopher Janney, who describes it as an "urban musical instrument." On display since it was selected as part of the Creative Stations Program in 1995, it's sparked joy for commuters day after day since then.

CREATIVITY AT NEW HEIGHTS

WHAT: *REACH* artwork

WHERE: 34th Street-Herald Square subway station, N/R line, Manhattan

COST: The cost of subway fare ($2.90, currently)

PRO TIP: If you're short, try waving a glove or newspaper in front of the artwork for some extra height.

At first it may look like an odd piece of ductwork, but this metal channel actually holds a musical surprise. Curious New Yorkers know art isn't just confined to museums in this city. For those who are paying attention, art is all around us.

This is just one of many pieces of art you can find in NYC's subway system, from paintings to mosaics to sculptures. Keep your eyes peeled for artwork all around thanks to MTA Arts & Design.

ENCRYPTED COMMENTS

Dying to get a secret off your chest?

Got a secret you're dying to spill? You can bury it deep in a grave at The Green-Wood Cemetery. An art installation called *Here Lie the Secrets of the Visitors of Green-Wood Cemetery* looks exactly like an obelisk-shaped tombstone with one key difference: This grave marker includes what looks like a mail slot. It's here that visitors can slip in a note containing their secret.

The artwork by Sophie Calle was installed at the cemetery in 2017 and is slated to be on view for at least 25 years, meaning you've got until 2042 to see it. It's not just public art, Green-Wood's Vice President of Education and Public Programming Harry J. Weil explains. The tombstone goes beyond the art world, allowing people to exorcise themselves of secrets they'd like to shed.

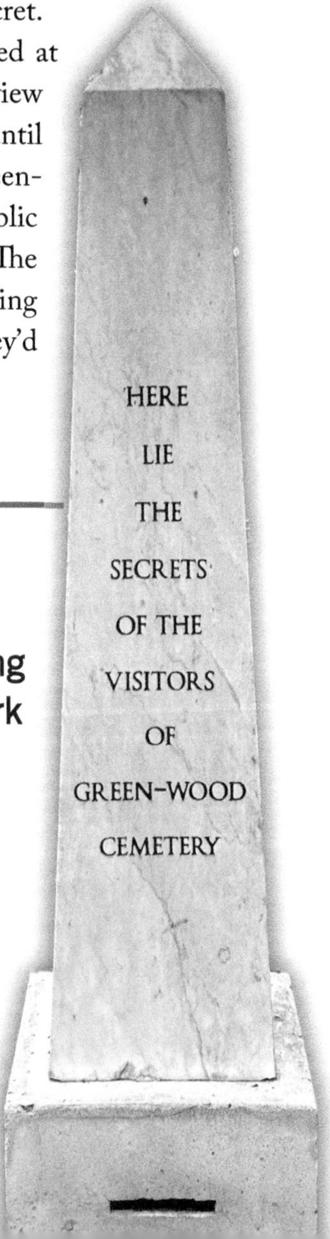

These aren't the only secrets buried at Green-Wood. The Victorians were known for encoding precious messages into the artwork on their gravestones. Green-Wood often hosts tours exploring those cryptic comments.

If you're planning to share a secret, be sure to bring a pen and paper, so you can jot down a note before dropping it into this obelisk. This tombstone artwork will be on view until early 2042, so you've got time to spill your secrets.

When someone slides a secret into the obelisk, it plunges down a shaft and lands in a container among tens of thousands of other secrets. There's still plenty of room for new secrets to be added to the pile—just remember to bring a pen and paper. Depositing a secret here can be an emotional experience, sometimes drawing tears to visitors' eyes. The artist has pledged to return each time the grave is filled to exhume and cremate all the secrets in a ceremonial bonfire.

TAKE IT TO THE GRAVE

WHAT: *Here Lie the Secrets of the Visitors of Green-Wood Cemetery*

WHERE: 500 25th St., Greenwood Heights, Brooklyn

COST: Free

PRO TIP: Enter through the main entrance at 25th Street; the installation is less than a 10-minute walk into the cemetery. Grab a cemetery map to help you find the right spot.

REMEMBERING LANGSTON HUGHES

Where can you pay tribute to an icon of the Harlem Renaissance?

Words from Langston Hughes's first published poem now mark his final resting place in Harlem, and all are welcome to visit and pay their respects. Hughes, known as Harlem's Poet Laureate, was an icon of the Harlem Renaissance movement, a cultural renaissance of Black art, music, and literature from 1918 to the mid-1930s.

Inside the Schomburg Center for Research in Black Culture, which is located in Harlem, Hughes's ashes are buried in a book-shaped urn beneath an art installation on the floor. The installation, called *Rivers,* draws upon Hughes's poem "The Negro Speaks of Rivers" and upon the tradition of African ritual ground markings known as cosmograms. The terrazzo artwork pulls lines from the poem, alongside rivers made in a turquoise blue hue. In the center, a fish-shaped icon bears the phrase "My soul has grown deep like the rivers" in brass lettering. His ashes lie beneath those words, the final line in Hughes's groundbreaking poem.

"MY SOUL HAS GROWN DEEP LIKE THE RIVERS"

WHAT: Langston Hughes's ashes at the Schomburg Center for Research in Black Culture

WHERE: 515 Malcolm X Blvd., Harlem, Manhattan

COST: Free

PRO TIP: The Schomburg Center often hosts exhibits, performances, and speeches, so keep an eye on their online calendar for events.

The artwork highlights important places in Hughes's life interwoven with key places in the life of Arturo A. Schomburg, for whom the center in Harlem is named. Schomburg, a Puerto Rican of African descent, was a writer, library curator, and collector of items related to African diasporan history and culture. Lifelines in the artwork show

This cosmogram is made from terrazzo with brick red and turquoise blue hues. Lifelines in the artwork highlight Puerto Rico, Missouri, and Harlem.

the men's places of birth (Puerto Rico for Schomburg and Missouri for Hughes) and where their paths crossed in Harlem.

Artist Houston Conwill created the piece in 1991. Since then it has served as a celebrated piece of art, a dance floor, and a peace memorial. *Rivers* strives to show the connections between people of diverse cultures and backgrounds, and between the past and the present.

Also visit the center's courtyard to see A Bench by the Road, a project by the Toni Morrison Society that marks important places in Black history and seeks to inspire conversations among those who sit on the bench.

SET IN STONE

Is this NYC's version of Stonehenge?

Thirteen stone monoliths sit along a wooded trail in Van Cortlandt Park. At first glance, it looks like they could be tombstones or some kind of mysterious Stonehenge installation. But these stones, set in one of the most remote areas of New York City, actually helped create one of the busiest buildings in the world.

Back in 1905, as the construction of Grand Central Terminal was underway, builders wanted to pick the best stone for the exterior walls of the train station. To do that, they placed 15 samples of granite, limestone, and marble in the park to determine how each one would hold up in a New York City winter. It's said to be the first time stone samples were evaluated by exposing them to the elements. Workers set the stones along the former Putnam branch of the New York Central Railroad, which ran passenger trains from 1870 to 1958. After five years, engineers studied the results and chose two stones for the train station: Indiana limestone for the upper portion and Connecticut's Stony Creek granite for the shop-front level.

These days, the Putnam railroad branch is now a nature trail, and the monoliths along it still endure. Visitors to the park can get up close with each stone, examining its veins, bumps, marks, and even stray bits of graffiti. Though builders chose two specific types of stone, all of the 13 samples on view have held up well over the

---

With 1,146 acres of green space, Van Cortlandt Park is one of the biggest parks in the city. It's also home to the oldest house in the Bronx, the borough's largest freshwater lake, and the country's first public golf course.

These monoliths seem to suddenly pop up alongside a wooded trail in the Bronx. Look closely at each one to notice how the stone has endured over the years. If you were building a train terminal, which one would you pick?

years. Two samples were either lost over the decades or planners decided to cut them from the list because they were so similar to other options. After you see the 13 remaining monoliths, keep an eye on the stonework next time you visit Grand Central. It might just look familiar.

DON'T TAKE IT FOR GRANITE

WHAT: Grand Central Stones

WHERE: Old Putnam Trail, Van Cortlandt Park, Bronx

COST: Free

PRO TIP: Plug "Grand Central Stones" into Google Maps to help you find the stones along the trail.

"TEAR DOWN THIS WALL"

Why is there a piece of Berlin in NYC?

For decades, East Germans living under communism faced an imposing concrete barrier that separated them from democracy in West Germany. For brave artists, this created a massive canvas. French artist Thierry Noir moved to Berlin in 1982, soon becoming the first artist to illegally paint miles of the Berlin Wall. His recognizable head drawings covered the wall in vibrant shades of red, yellow, and blue.

The wall was finally dismantled in 1989, freeing millions of people who had been held captive under communism. While much of its concrete was ground up to create roadways, some pieces of the wall found new homes in America.

One piece, titled *Homage to Liberty* by Thierry Noir himself, now stands in Lower Manhattan. The 12-foot-tall, 8-foot-wide, 2.75-ton section of the Berlin Wall was donated in 2004 on the 15th anniversary of the wall's demolition. It once stood in downtown Berlin between Potsdamer Platz and Leipziger Platz as part of the inner wall designed to prevent East Germans from escaping. The artwork bears a tall, green face with red lips and hair. On the other side, there's a wispy white and gold painting of a face by artist Kiddy Citny.

FROM BERLIN WITH LOVE

WHAT: A piece of the Berlin Wall

WHERE: Kowsky Plaza, 393 South End Ave., Lower Manhattan

COST: Free

PRO TIP: Kowsky Plaza is also a popular spot for pups, as the park's dog run includes space for canines to jump, perch, and splash.

This piece by Thierry Noir titled Homage to Liberty *(at left) has stood in Lower Manhattan since 2004. The scale of the artwork shows just how large the Berlin Wall was; this piece stood in downtown Berlin between Potsdamer Platz and Leipziger Platz.*

The German Consulate donated this section of the wall to the Hugh L. Carey Battery Park City Authority to recognize the park's commitment to education through public art. The park authority says the artwork stands as a symbol of the strength of democracy.

There's another section of the Berlin Wall at the United Nations Plaza, which you can see on the garden tour of the facility.

A SOMBER CORRIDOR

Where can you walk through part of the original World Trade Center?

The terrorist attacks of September 11, 2001, collapsed the Twin Towers into smoldering rubble, killing 2,753 people and demolishing part of Lower Manhattan. The horrific event leveled what was once a bustling site of commerce that attracted 70,000 commuters and tourists every day. But a piece of daily life before 9/11 still exists, tucked along a subway corridor just off the E train.

The E train entrance/exit connecting to the Oculus (on the North Concourse, Balcony Level C1) looks noticeably different from the rest of the area. The doors, overhead lighting, and tan travertine floor don't match the more updated design aesthetic of the building. Instead, this entrance looks just as it did before 9/11. It still continues in its role as a passageway for commuters and visitors, thanks to the Port Authority of New York & New Jersey's preservation efforts.

A gray metal door in the hallway bears several markings in orange spray paint. These were made by search-and-rescue teams in the aftermath of the attacks. One marking reads "913," indicating that a search occurred there on September 13, 2001. An "X" in a painted square meant the area was dangerous at that time. Another symbol shows that the search was completed by FEMA's Massachusetts task force.

While you're in the area, also visit the 9/11 Memorial plaza. Look for the Survivor Tree, a Callery pear tree that was severely damaged during the attacks. NYC Parks staff nursed it back to health, and it stands today as a symbol of resilience.

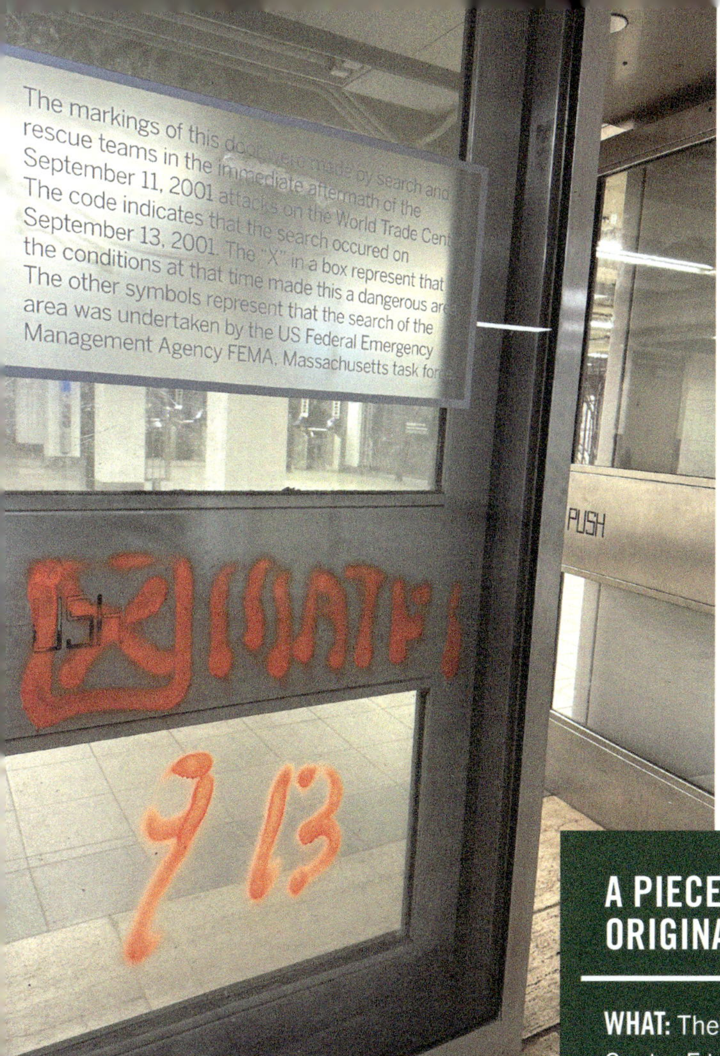

Commuters are often in a rush to catch their trains, but slow down here and take a moment to remember the victims of the 9/11 terrorist attacks. Notice how the flooring, lighting, and doors look a bit different—that will indicate you've found the site.

Walking through this area feels deeply emotional. It's impossible not to think about the people who passed through that same hallway on their way to work on September 11, 2001, unaware of the fate that would soon befall them. Remember them as you visit.

A PIECE OF THE ORIGINAL WTC

WHAT: The original World Trade Center E train entrance

WHERE: The E train entrance/exit connecting to the Oculus at 50 Church St., Financial District, Manhattan

COST: Free

PRO TIP: Go to North Concourse, Balcony Level C1 in the Oculus, and proceed toward the E train. You'll see it before you get to the train fare turnstiles.

A MEDITATIVE OASIS

How can you see a piece of China without ever leaving NYC?

In a verdant part of Staten Island, a serene scene transports visitors thousands of miles away to China. The New York Chinese Scholar's Garden is one of just two authentic classical outdoor Chinese gardens in the United States. Find this outdoor oasis at Snug Harbor Cultural Center & Botanic Garden.

Tall bamboo plants spring up along the winding stone paths leading to the garden. The wind rustles through the soaring stands of plants, creating a welcoming song. Walk by koi-filled ponds and flowering trees to enter the garden's ivy-covered walls. Inside you'll find open-air pavilions, corridors, and rooms, each one imbued with sacred meaning.

Be sure to look up to notice the ornate architectural features, such as flying eaves, and to look down to spot detailed stone mosaics in the floors. Artful calligraphy decorates the space, indicating names of different areas in the garden, like "The Garden of Poetic Pleasure." Gaze through the circular Moon Gate, which symbolizes the completeness of the universe and offers exquisite views of the garden. In a Chinese Scholar's Garden, plants are arranged not just by their appearance but by their meanings, as well. Yellow Grove Bamboo, for example, is a symbol of the scholar: flexible but strong. Towering rock sculptures resemble mountains that inspired the poetry and paintings of Confucian, Buddhist, and Taoist monks.

SCHOLARLY SPOT

WHAT: The New York Chinese Scholar's Garden at Snug Harbor Cultural Center & Botanical Garden

WHERE: 1000 Richmond Ter., Randall Manor, Staten Island

COST: $5

PRO TIP: Check Snug Harbor's website for opening dates and times, which vary seasonally.

Find The New York Chinese Scholar's Garden at Snug Harbor in Staten Island. It's one of just two authentic classical outdoor Chinese gardens in the United States.

While the design is based on Ming Dynasty gardens dating back to 1368-1644, this one was created in 1999 by a team of 40 experts in Suzhou, China. All of the materials, from bridges to roof tiles, were fabricated in China, then brought to the United States where the team from China spent six months completing the construction. For decades, it has offered a place for all to reflect, study, and meditate.

Inside the garden, you might notice that the bridges and paths frequently zigzag. The design provides ever-changing vantage points to experience the garden—plus, Chinese philosophers believed zigzagging paths would throw off evil spirits.

TALKING ABOUT A REVOLUTION

Why do those fence posts look a little off-kilter?

At the very bottom tip of Manhattan, a small park holds centuries of history. Indigenous people used the land as a council ground. It's even where the Dutch "purchased" Manhattan in 1626. After taking control of the property, the Dutch used it as a parade ground, a meeting place, a cattle market, and a lawn bowling spot, leading to the park's name of Bowling Green.

By 1770, now under British rule, a gilded lead statue went up of Britain's King George III on horseback, and an iron fence surrounded the park shortly thereafter. But a revolution was on the way.

On July 9, 1776, after the first public reading of the Declaration of Independence in New York, citizens toppled the king's monument and

A FEISTY FENCE

WHAT: Bowling Green fence

WHERE: 24 Broadway, Financial District, Manhattan

COST: Free

PRO TIP: While you're there, visit the nearby National Museum of the American Indian (it's free to enter).

The park is called Bowling Green because settlers used to use it for lawn bowling.

dragged it up Broadway. They sent the royal statue to Connecticut to be melted and recast as ammunition.

While in the park, revolutionaries also lopped the crowns off of the iron fence posts that surrounded Bowling Green. Though the crowns are gone, the fence itself remains and is now a New York City landmark. If you look closely at the fence posts, you will notice that some look uneven, as if they were hastily excised in the furor of a budding democracy's beginnings.

As for the demolished king statue, loyalists saved some pieces, including the horse's tail, and bits of it remain at the New-York Historical Society.

To find the fence, don't get distracted by the Charging Bull statue everyone takes a photo of. Instead, keep walking and head into Bowling Green.

You'll need to look closely to see this secret. Notice how these fence posts look a little uneven? There's a revolutionary reason.

SPOT THIS SPOT

What's that dirty spot in Grand Central?

Even if it can be hard to see constellations in Manhattan, the stars always dazzle at Grand Central Terminal. A massive cerulean mural covers the domed ceiling of the terminal to depict the zodiac with 12 gold-leaf constellations and 2,500 stars; 59 of the stars are even lit with LED bulbs. Hundreds of thousands of people walk beneath this behemoth mural every day, but very few likely notice the dirty patch on the ceiling.

That gray spot tells the tumultuous history of the terminal, which barely evaded demolition. The resplendent train depot opened in 1913 and prospered for years, but in 1967 a developer wanted to demolish parts of the building. City leaders, including Jacqueline Kennedy Onassis, pushed back against the proposal and secured Grand Central as a National Historic Landmark. But the station was crumbling and needed plenty of preservation work.

After years of buildup from pollution, the azure ceiling was hidden under a layer of soot and grime. Preservationists meticulously cleaned the mural over a six-month period in the 1990s, finally returning it to its original glory. They left a tiny rectangular patch untouched for historic documentation, essentially providing evidence of the conditions for future preservationists. As for everybody else, the dirty spot creates a stunning before and after. It also offers a stark reminder of the preservationists' efforts and the importance of preserving history.

A TRULY DIRTY STORY

WHAT: A dirty mark on the Grand Central ceiling

WHERE: Grand Central Terminal Main Concourse, 89 E 42nd St., Midtown East, Manhattan

COST: Free

PRO TIP: While you're looking up, also look for a round hole. This hole was drilled into the ceiling to anchor a rocket displayed there in 1957 during the Space Race era.

Yes, the constellations are backward. Some say it was a mistake, while others insist the artist's point of view was intentionally from the heavens to the earth.

To find the 9-inch-by-18-inch stained section, look toward Cancer the crab, whose claw will point you in the right direction.

While this venue is one of the most iconic in New York City, very few know to pay attention to the dirty patch overhead that tells the building's history.

WORD ON THE STREET

Why does that street sign look a little different?

If you're walking through the Jackson Heights neighborhood in Queens, there's a street sign that might just stop you in your tracks. The sign for 35th Avenue looks a little odd. Next to each letter, a tiny number appears in subscript. A one shows up next to the "T," a four by the "H," and so on. While this sign might look like a misprint to many, Scrabble players will immediately recognize it as an homage to the beloved word game. The sign, which appears at the intersection of 35th Avenue and 81st Street in front of a church, marks the birthplace of Scrabble.

An architect by the name of Alfred M. Butts is credited with creating the board game in 1931. Butts designed the education building connected to Community United Methodist Church of Jackson Heights. In that very building, he perfected the game with help from his wife, Nina, and his church congregation. Church records from the mid-1930s even show reservations for games of Scrabble in the church's social hall. Today, a plaque on the brown brick church annex credits his achievement.

With its unusual lettering, this street sign in Queens is unlike any other in New York City. For a game all about words, very few words commemorate this important spot. Don't miss the small plaque on the side of the church.

A SCRABBLE STORY

WHAT: The birthplace of Scrabble

WHERE: 35th Ave. and 81st St., Jackson Heights, Queens

COST: Free

PRO TIP: Find the street sign at the intersection in front of the church. The plaque is located along the church annex on 35th Avenue.

The designer first called the game Lexiko, then made some tweaks and called it Criss-Cross Words. Several years later, as it surged in popularity, the game became known as Scrabble. That game, first created in the Great Depression and honed with help from New Yorkers, has become a worldwide phenomenon, and it all dates back to Jackson Heights in Queens.

By the way, "35th Avenue" counts for 14 points in a Scrabble game. Not too shabby.

For many years the published history of Scrabble was murky, until a Jackson Heights resident set the record straight in the 1990s and put its Queens origins back on the map.

TIME TRAVEL TO THE 1600S

How can you step into Colonial-era life?

Amid Lower Manhattan's towering skyscrapers, futuristic electric cars, and passersby swiping on their smartphones, those who are willing to take a moment to look down can transport themselves from the modern trappings of the 21st century to a simpler time in the 17th century.

Beneath a pane of glass in the sidewalk along Pearl Street, you can catch a glimpse of New York City during the 1600s. On view are sections of the wall from the Lovelace Tavern, which operated between 1670 and 1706. Led by Francis Lovelace, the second English governor of New York, the building served as a temporary city hall around 1697. In the basement of the tavern, archaeologists discovered wine bottles and clay tobacco pipes.

Also on view is a well that dates back to the early 1700s. This well was located on the property of the Phillipse family, one of the most prominent families in colonial New York, and it provided water to the people who lived on that block. After wells went out of use, families often used them as a makeshift garbage dump, which provided researchers with lots of fascinating finds.

During an excavation in 1979 and 1980, archaeologists discovered more about what's called the Stadt Hus (Dutch City Hall) block. In 1653, when the land was under Dutch rule, they established their city hall in a traditional building with a stepped gable. It served as

HISTORY BENEATH YOUR FEET

WHAT: Portal down to Old New York

WHERE: 63 Pearl St., Financial District, Manhattan

COST: Free

PRO TIP: Go on a sunny day. It's tough to see into the portal when the glass is wet.

This exhibition in Lower Manhattan serves as a tangible reminder that history is always beneath our feet. Beneath this glass, you'll see pieces of the city's history dating back to the 1600s.

a municipal building under Dutch and English rule until 1697, when it was deemed unsafe. Cream-colored pavers show the outline of where the Stadt Hus would've been located.

This was the site of the first large-scale archaeological excavation in New York City. It proved that significant archaeological remnants can be found even in developed urban areas.

SHOP SMALL—LITERALLY

In cramped Manhattan, just how tiny can a store get?

Space is at a premium in Manhattan. On an island home to 1.6 million people, folks around here tend to get creative in small spaces. But very few are quite as creative as the couple behind MoonLab 42, a 58-inch art shop in Harlem.

Though it feels more like a hallway, this concept store wedged between two apartment buildings in Harlem packs plenty of wonderful wares into its narrow frame. Inside the shop, you'll find vinyl records, tote bags, candles, shirts, cards, soaps, zines, sculptures, art prints, and lots more. It's the perfect off-the-beaten-path spot to find a gift for a friend or for yourself.

The idea began when art fairs and shows paused amid the pandemic. In response, local couple Ruso Margishvili and John Holden gathered art and design pieces from their friends and family and displayed them in a pop-up at a Harlem coffee shop. From there, the concept blossomed into the creation of the storefront, MoonLab 42.

The petite MoonLab 42 sits between two tall apartment buildings in Harlem. See if you can identify it in this photo. Photo courtesy of Ivane Katamashvili.

Despite its small footprint, the shop is smartly designed to fit plenty of artful items. Photo courtesy of Dimitri Mais.

A TINY TREASURE TROVE

WHAT: MoonLab 42

WHERE: 405 W 145th St., Sugar Hill, Harlem

COST: Free to visit

PRO TIP: MoonLab 42 often hosts parties that spill out of the store onto the sidewalk. Check their website for more info.

The store's co-owners carefully curate the items on the shelves, drawing from a vast array of artists in the United States and the country of Georgia. Then, they find a temporary home for each piece in their Mary Poppins–bag of a store, until each item finds its way to its permanent home.

The store's name is a testament to the co-owners' late-night candle making in the moonlight, and it also alludes to the shop Margishvili's family ran in her home country of Georgia.

A SOBERING SCULPTURE

How can a fountain double as political propaganda?

Union Square Park is packed with historical sculptures and monuments. George Washington sits astride a horse in a triumphant pose. Revolutionary General Marquis de Lafayette brandishes a sword. A peaceful Mohandas Gandhi strolls through a garden.

But one monument doesn't quite fit the mold. Dubbed the James Fountain, this 19-foot-tall sculpture depicts a pious-looking woman holding a baby and leading another child by the hand. The child helps her carry a jug of water while they look lovingly at one another. The subjects perch atop an ornate pedestal with floral garlands and lions.

The fountain dates back to 1881, making it one of the oldest sculptures in New York City's park system. It's also among the few remaining temperance fountains in the nation.

Philanthropist Daniel Willis James donated the fountain to promote public public health and the virtue of charity. Many fountains popped up in this era to celebrate the new, fresh Croton Aqueduct, which itself was a major advance as New Yorkers previously relied on often-contaminated well water. At one time, cups even hung from the fountain for passersby to get a drink; it is no longer a working drinking fountain today.

SPOUTING POLITICS AND RELIGION

WHAT: James Fountain, a temperance fountain

WHERE: West side of Union Square Park, Union Square West between East 15th and East 16th Sts., Manhattan

COST: Free

PRO TIP: Stop by when the Greenmarket, a massive farmers market, is open.

Though less ornate, there's another temperance sculpture in Tompkins Square Park. It's designed in a canopy style and inscribed with the words "Faith, Hope, Charity, and Temperance."

But the fountain was also intended to teach a lesson about religion—and the temperance movement, the political campaign that urged moderation in alcoholic consumption and eventually prohibition. James was sympathetic to the temperance cause, and fountains like these offered cool drinking water as an alternative to booze. The temperance movement didn't last, but the sculpture has endured the decades.

A German sculptor named Karl Adolf Donndorf created the Union Square sculpture. He labored over it, trying to make it a museum-quality work with meticulous attention to detail.

BEWITCHING ART

Is there really a witch in Central Park?

The jury's still out on whether Central Park is haunted and whether trolls live under any of the park's many bridges. But there's definitely a witch in the park, and she presides over the area near the Bethesda Terrace and the Mall.

The witch is one of the many intricate carvings in the railings leading up to the Mall. Central Park's renowned co-designer Calvert Vaux envisioned the decorative carvings to depict the passage of time. The witch, naturally, represents nighttime, alongside a miniature 1800s cityscape depicting Halloween. In the artwork, the witch wears a cape and a pointy hat while flying on a broomstick. In the background, there's a jack-o'-lantern, a creepy tree, and a stone house.

In addition to portraying Halloween spirit year-round, the artwork also pays homage to the Irish immigrants and workers who helped to build the park. Back when Bethesda Terrace was built in the 1800s, the holiday was tied to Irish culture.

WITCHY WOMAN

WHAT: Witch carving

WHERE: Between Bethesda Terrace and the Mall, Central Park, Manhattan

COST: Free

PRO TIP: Also walk down to the Bethesda Fountain to see the beloved *Angel of the Waters* sculpture.

Architect Jacob Wrey Mould designed the witch, along with many other pieces that depict the four seasons. Look for his other detailed carvings, such as tulips, a bird's nest, pine cones, and an owl, along Bethesda Terrace.

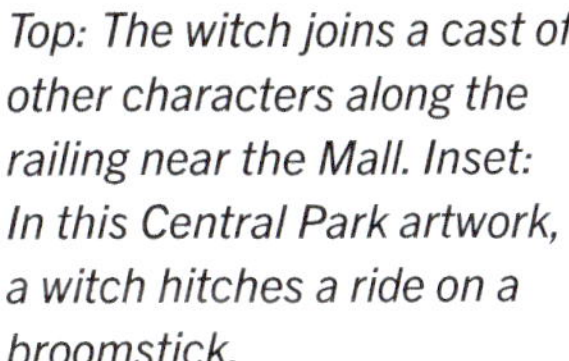

Top: The witch joins a cast of other characters along the railing near the Mall. Inset: In this Central Park artwork, a witch hitches a ride on a broomstick.

Though the carvings are staggeringly beautiful, it's easy to breeze right past them while biking, running, or strolling through the park's lush foliage. Even Vaux himself likely wouldn't have minded. He's said to have told a newspaper reporter that even the beautiful terrace should be subordinate to the landscape: "Nature first, second, and third—architecture after awhile."

TRUE CRIME IN EARLY AMERICA

Where can you see the site that led to America's first murder trial?

Inside this typical clothing store, shoppers paw through clothing racks, try on jackets, and check price tags. Little do they know there's something eerie afoot. In the basement of 129 Spring St., which is currently home to a retail store, sits a large brick well. Seemingly just a relic of the past, it's unmarked and wouldn't attract much attention if you didn't know what you were looking for.

However, this well was the site of a grisly death in 1799, which led to the first murder trial in the United States and a major test for the fledgling justice system. You've likely never heard of the victim, a young woman named Elma Sands. But you've probably heard of the accused's attorneys—Aaron Burr and Alexander Hamilton.

A GRISLY SITE WITH JUDICIAL IMPORTANCE

WHAT: Manhattan Well murder site

WHERE: 129 Spring St. (currently a retail store), Soho, Manhattan

COST: Free

PRO TIP: Head downstairs to the basement level of the store to find the well.

Here's the backstory: Elma was dating a prominent, wealthy man named Levi Weeks. She said she was going to secretly get married to him on the night of December 22, 1799. Instead, she disappeared. Her body was found with bruises and wounds on

---

The case is even referenced in the hit musical *Hamilton.* Turn on the song "Non-Stop" and listen for the lyrics about Levi Weeks.

This well is unmarked, but it has a remarkable history. Find it in the basement of a retail store in Soho.

January 2, 1800, at the bottom of the Manhattan Well. A grand jury indicted Weeks for her murder. But at trial, after hearing arguments from Burr and Hamilton, the jury acquitted him after just five minutes of deliberation. Even though he went free, the court of public opinion wasn't happy with the decision, and New Yorkers ostracized Weeks until he left the city for Mississippi. The case was never solved.

Given how quickly buildings in New York City change, it's shocking that the well still exists, especially considering it doesn't have protected landmark status.

This well was the site of a grisly murder in 1799.

HEART OF THE OCEAN

Where can you pay tribute to a real-life Titanic love story?

While Kate and Leo present a gripping love story in the movie *Titanic*, there's another couple whose enduring love makes viewers reach for the tissues. It's the older couple who clasp hands in bed while the frigid water rises around them in their cabin. It turns out, that story from the movie is actually based on a real couple with New York City roots.

Isidor and Ida Straus booked a last-minute ticket on the Titanic to come home to New York after a vacation in Europe. Isidor, a former congressman, was a co-owner of R.H. Macy & Co. along with his brother. The affluent couple traveled with a butler and maid and were able to secure a first-class cabin.

After the massive boat struck the iceberg, Ida was offered a spot in a lifeboat, but she refused to go without her husband. Isidor, meanwhile, was offered a place on another lifeboat but wouldn't get in without her. She said to him: "Isidor, we have been together for all these years. Where you go, I go." They insisted their maid, Ellen Bird, get onto the lifeboat. Ida handed her fur coat to Ellen, saying she'd have no use for it anymore. The couple was last seen sitting together, arm in arm, on the boat's deck. Ellen survived; Isidor Straus's body was recovered and buried in New York, while Ida was never found.

A brass memorial plaque with images of the couple hangs inside Macy's. It reads, "Their lives were beautiful and their deaths glorious.

There are several other Titanic tributes to see, including the Titanic Memorial Lighthouse in the Seaport. In the Battery, there's a monument to wireless operators lost at sea, which mentions an operator lost on the Titanic.

Enter through these doors on 34th Street to find the memorial.

A LASTING LOVE STORY

WHAT: Titanic memorial plaque to the Strauses

WHERE: Macy's Herald Square, 151 W 34th St., Manhattan

COST: Free

PRO TIP: Enter through the 34th Street Memorial Entrance; look for the ornate statues that adorn the exterior of the building on 34th Street.

This plaque in Macy's tells a Titanic love story.

This tablet is the voluntary token of sorrowing employees." The plaque lists their birth dates and their death date—April 15, 1912.

To see another memorial to the Strauses, head uptown to Straus Park (106th and Broadway) on the Upper West Side. The parklet features flowers, benches, a sculpture, and an inscription remembering the couple, which reads in part: "Lovely and pleasant were they in their lives and in their death they were not divided."

BUG OUT

Where can you ride atop a praying mantis?

No matter your age, riding a carousel always feels magical—the horse statues decked out in their finest saddles, the sprightly organ music, and the air of vintage enchantment. The Bronx Zoo takes the fantastical experience to new levels. Their carousel forgoes the traditional horse motif and instead features an assortment of insects.

Sixty-four lifelike sculptures of caterpillars, grasshoppers, praying mantises, cicadas, beetles, and more serve as the seating on this carousel. The carousel also offers a few bench seats for ADA accessibility—or for those who may be too creeped out by the creepy crawlers. Fair warning that one of those benches is shaped like a giant pile of dung accompanied by a dung beetle. On the center of the carousel, visitors can watch an illustration showing the life cycle of a butterfly, from caterpillar to beautiful winged insect.

The Bug Carousel dates back to 2005 when it debuted alongside the opening of the Bronx Zoo's Butterfly Garden to expand experiences about the value of insects. It's said to be the first "all-bug carousel" in the world, an accolade that's pretty fly. Other parts of the carousel, like its LED lights and golden poles, mimic a more traditional carousel.

TO BEE OR NOT TO BEE

WHAT: Bronx Zoo bug carousel

WHERE: 2300 Southern Blvd., Bronx

COST: Visit bronxzoo.com for pricing, as it changes seasonally.

PRO TIP: Don't worry if there's a line. A series of signs with facts about bugs will keep kids entertained while they wait.

Featuring bugs instead of horses, this isn't your typical carousel. This Bronx Zoo spectacle delights kids of all ages.

The carousel operates year-round; in the winter, sliding glass doors enclose the attraction, so you can hitch a ride on a praying mantis no matter the weather.

Each bug was painted with attention to detail. The praying mantis wears a vivid green color, the bumble bee looks practically fuzzy, and the beetles appear almost too creepy to touch.

FEELING FIZZY

What's the story behind seltzer?

From La Croix to White Claw, seltzer is having a moment. But in New York City, this bubbly beverage has been a longtime favorite.

The Brooklyn Seltzer Museum, a new addition to the city's cadre of quirky museums, explores the history of the drink and explains the delicious details of the seltzer-making process. The museum operates in Brooklyn Seltzer Boys, which is the last old-fashioned seltzer factory in New York and one of the few remaining in the country. The family-run business dates back to 1953 when it was run by Moe Gomberg who then called it Gomberg Seltzer Works; these days, it's got a new name, a new warehouse, and a new leader, Alex Gomberg, Moe's great-grandson.

Teaming up with Barry Joseph (museum designer and author of *Seltzertopia*), the two transformed a standard warehouse into a fascinating non-profit museum. Whether on a tour or at a special weekend event, you'll see the seltzer-making process up-close and in action. The staff carefully clean and fill vintage glass bottles (siphons), many of which were handblown in Czechoslovakia in the early 1900s and continue to be circulated today to households, restaurants, and bars around the region. The process employs an ancient workhorse of a machine that fills bottle after bottle under the watchful eye of the Brooklyn Seltzer Boys.

In addition to learning about the process—from plain tap water through triple filtration, then chilling, carbonation, and bottling—visitors can enjoy some all-ages fun. There's a digital scavenger

POP BY SOMETIME

WHAT: Brooklyn Seltzer Museum

WHERE: 474 Hemlock St., Cypress Hills, Brooklyn

COST: $25

PRO TIP: Public tours are offered weekly on a limited basis, and private tours are also available with advance notice; be sure to book online in advance.

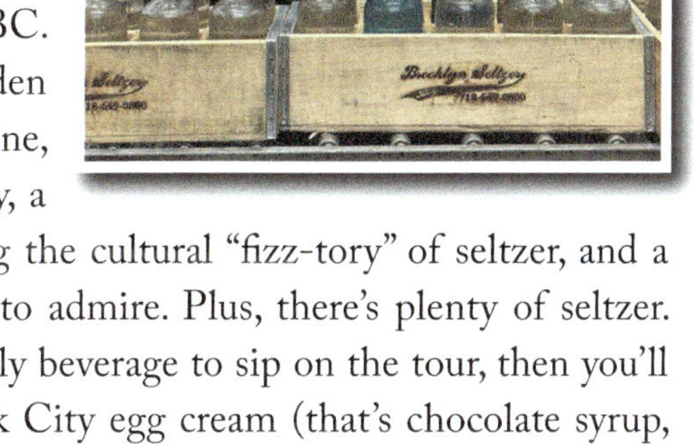

On a tour, you'll get to see the seltzer-making process in action. These old-school machines still get the job done day after day.

hunt, which encourages a deep understanding of the seltzer timeline dating back to 400 BC. Also expect photo ops, a wooden puzzle of the production line, 3D models of the machinery, a 24-foot-long mural depicting the cultural "fizz-tory" of seltzer, and a display of vintage glassware to admire. Plus, there's plenty of seltzer. You'll get a glass of the bubbly beverage to sip on the tour, then you'll get to try a classic New York City egg cream (that's chocolate syrup, whole milk, and seltzer) at the end of the tour. Cheers to that.

Tours include a super cool slow-motion photo opportunity where you'll get to spray seltzer at a loved one (through a piece of plexiglass).

THE TRIANGLE TRAGEDY

Where can you pay tribute to victims of the Triangle Shirtwaist Factory fire?

IN MEMORY OF THE 146

WHAT: Triangle Fire Memorial

WHERE: The Brown Building, 23 Washington Pl., Greenwich Village, Manhattan

COST: Free

PRO TIP: Gaze into the reflective glass at hip level to see each victim's name, and take a moment to remember their lives

As flames burst through the upper levels of a 10-story garment factory in Greenwich Village on March 25, 1911, workers were faced with few options. The exit door was locked. A fire escape had collapsed. Rescue ladders weren't tall enough to reach them. With flames and smoke closing in around them, many decided to jump out the windows, dying as they crashed onto the sidewalk below.

The horrific carnage—146 workers dead, many of them immigrant women—finally secured the protections and rights the workers had been advocating for before their untimely deaths. The Triangle Shirtwaist Factory Fire in 1911 remained New York's worst workplace disaster until the 9/11 terrorist attacks.

Despite damage sustained in the fire, the building still stands at the corner of Greene Street and Washington Place. Today, it's an academic building for New York University. Until 2023, only a small plaque honoring the victims indicated the building's history.

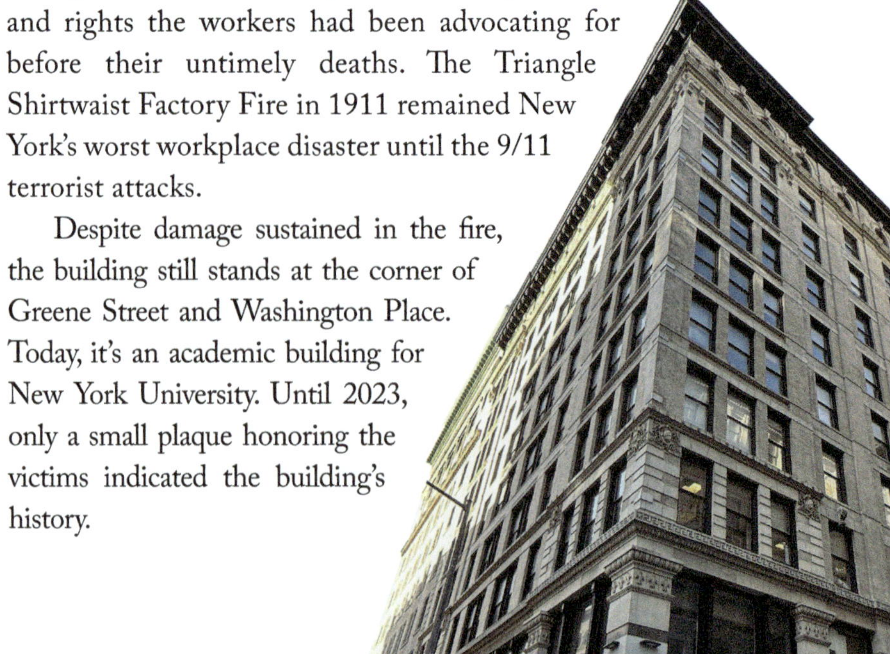

More than a century after this horrific incident, a powerful memorial remembers the victims of the Triangle Shirtwaist Factory Fire. The Brown Building still stands, and today it's used as an academic building.

But at long last, there's now a stunning monument paying tribute to the victims' memories. The monument lists all of the victims' names, each one cut into a piece of metal mounted onto the building.

The memorial also includes quotes from those on the scene during the fire. One quote from a blouse maker reads: "There, smashed on the sidewalk, were the beautiful faces of those who were my neighbors at the machines." A fire department official is quoted as saying: "I thought they would come down one at a time. They came down with arms entwined—three and even four together."

The Remember the Triangle Fire Coalition maintains a map of all known burial sites for victims of the fire: rememberthetrianglefire.org/learn/names

UNDERGROUND ART

What's that weird sound in Times Square?

YOU'VE GOT TO HEAR THIS

WHAT: Times Square sound art

WHERE: Broadway Pedestrian Plaza between 45th and 46th Sts. (between Broadway and 7th Ave.), Times Square, Manhattan

COST: Free

PRO TIP: The sound runs 24/7, but it's best to visit early in the morning when there's less background noise.

In the cacophony that is Times Square, where taxis honk their horns, pedicab drivers blast "Empire State of Mind," construction trucks beep, sirens wail, and tourists chatter, it can be hard to hear yourself think. And yet, once you tune your ears to the unusual frequency of this secret audio artwork, you won't be able to pass through Times Square without hearing it.

Head to the Broadway Pedestrian Plaza between 45th and 46th Streets, stand atop the metal grate in the sidewalk and listen. Eventually, you might start to hear something odd, like the tone of a bell ringing or the rumbling of a distant subway train or the sound of someone running their finger along the rim of a crystal glass. That hard-to-place sound is, in fact, auditory artwork by the late Max Neuhaus.

The installation debuted in 1977 and ran until 1992, when the artist could no longer care for it. It vanished until 2002 when Dia Art Foundation worked with MTA Arts & Design and the Times Square Alliance to reinstate it.

You can't really see this artwork. You'll just have to listen. Simply titled Times Square, the droning sound intentionally blends in with the noise of the area.

Simply called Times Square, the droning sound is intended to blend in with the environment. Neuhaus was a skilled percussionist who wanted to make his work available for all to hear—or, at least, for those willing to listen. He insisted that the site remain unmarked, hidden beneath a typical grate. There's nothing to see here—just to hear.

Though the artwork makes for a fascinating and even meditative experience, very few passersby actually stop to listen. Instead, they rush past scrolling on their phones, chatting with friends, or just trying to push through the throngs of people. Many wear headphones, their ears buried in music or a podcast that drowns out the noise of the city.

The brilliance of Times Square is that it asks people to tune into this specific frequency, and in turn, it tunes us into the environment around us.

REMEMBERING "AN GORTA MÓR"

Where is there a piece of Ireland in NYC?

Three thousand miles across an ocean, a house from Ireland has found a home in New York City. A simple stone cottage dating back to the mid-1800s stands as part of the Irish Hunger Memorial in Lower Manhattan. The famine-era home expresses solidarity with Irish expats in America from those who stayed behind in their home country.

The powerful yet understated memorial designed by Brian Tolle fills a half-acre site near the Hudson River in remembrance of the one-and-a-half million lives lost during the famine. Upon encountering the site, you'll first notice a tall cantilevered shelf so high you can walk beneath it. Illuminated quotes fill the wall beneath the shelf, focusing on both the Great Irish Famine (known in Ireland as An Gorta Mór) as well as other instances of hunger. One quote, for

A PIECE OF IRELAND IN MANHATTAN

WHAT: Irish Hunger Memorial

WHERE: North End Ave. and Vesey St., Lower Manhattan

COST: Free

PRO TIP: While the memorial is on view year-round, it's best to visit in warmer months when the plants are at their greenest. The memorial's wild irises bloom in the spring, and wild roses last all summer and into the fall.

The Irish Hunger Memorial is located in Lower Manhattan along the Hudson River. The memorial's walls are filled with powerful quotes about hunger.

example, from former New York Governor George Pataki reads: "We have to think back, reflect, understand, learn how the Great Starvation of 1845–1852 could have happened, not simply to be in the position to understand history, but to prevent it from happening again."

After reading the quotes, pass through a stone hallway to the historic cottage, which was donated by a family in western Ireland, then painstakingly reconstructed in New York. From there, follow a winding path through a rugged landscape designed to look like Ireland. Lush plants, including some native to Ireland, fill the verdant landscape, along with stones from each of Ireland's 32 counties.

A climb to the top of the memorial presents a stunning visual of the Statue of Liberty and Ellis Island, a view that millions of Irish immigrants would have seen as they arrived in America, many forced to immigrate because of the famine.

Look for a QR code on-site, which you can scan for a full map of all the county stones, from Armagh to Donegal to Wicklow.

LET US SPRAY

Where can you find the city's greatest graffiti?

Even though graffiti is technically illegal, it's easy to spot tags all over New York City. There's one place, however, that takes spray paint to museum-quality levels. That's the Graffiti Hall of Fame in Manhattan's East Harlem neighborhood, also known as El Barrio in honor of its Puerto Rican population. These walls welcome "strictly kings and better." In graffiti parlance, that means it's a place for the best of the best to showcase their artwork.

Colorful graffiti brightens up this concrete wall along a schoolyard, and the artwork changes often so it's worth stopping by frequently. Oversized block letters spelling out HARLEM serve as a backdrop along the walls; artists color in each letter with their own visions. Past pieces have included eyes, stars, a boom box, a tribute to the late rapper Big Pun, and, of course, incredible lettering.

Graffiti, also known as style writing, originated in New York City as part of the hip-hop movement. Community activist

STRICTLY KINGS

WHAT: Graffiti Hall of Fame

WHERE: Park Ave. at E 106th St., East Harlem, Manhattan

COST: Free, except during special events.

PRO TIP: There are two walls to see. The first is in the playground of the Jackie Robinson Educational Complex, which is only open on weekends. The second, located on Park Avenue at East 106th, is open to visitors anytime.

Mark your calendar for the Graffiti Hall of Fame's annual event on the last weekend in August, which welcomes artists from around the globe to participate in a paint jam festival. Entry is usually $10.

The Graffiti Hall of Fame in East Harlem is a designated space for expert artists to show their skills. Take a moment to appreciate the impeccable artistry, like the shadowing on the letters.

Ray Rodriguez ("Sting Ray") founded the Graffiti Hall of Fame in 1980 as a place for graffiti artists and local kids to practice their skills. Nowadays, because of the relatively small space, artists must compete for a spot on the walls, which are maintained by TATS CRU, a group of professional muralists from the Bronx.

OH, RATS

Why are rats crawling up this building?

Rats are just a part of life around NYC, but usually they're seen scurrying across a sidewalk, not ensconced in architecture. At the Graybar Building, though, rats are a work of art.

An overhang juts out from the Art Deco office tower with a series of supports affixing it to the building. A sculpture of a rat climbs up each of those cables, which are intended to look like ropes on a ship. Unfortunately for the rats, though, they're stymied by a funnel-shaped rat guard, made to look just like the actual ones used on boats. The designer wanted the ropes and rats to evoke a maritime theme, given the city's history as a major seaport.

Once you spot the climbing rats, look closer to see more sculpted rats surrounding a porthole design on the building. Those rats symbolize the creatures who somehow made their way onto the boat. Look even closer and you'll spot some albatrosses in the design.

RAT RACE

WHAT: Rat sculptures

WHERE: Graybar Building, Lexington Ave. between 43rd and 44th Sts., Manhattan

COST: Free

PRO TIP: Try not to visit during rush hour as the sidewalks get pretty chaotic at that time of day.

Once the largest office tower in the world, the Graybar Building has its very own ZIP code: 10170.

Though these rats have been under scaffolding for quite a while, you can still catch a glimpse of them. New York City may be waging a war against rats, but these ones are works of art.

Back when the building was completed in 1927, the designer "tried to symbolize the fact that the Graybar Building was the focal point of the country's greatest maritime and railroad center," per a 1955 *New York Times* article. The building stands next to Grand Central, still a major railroad hub. Over the years, the rats disappeared, but they were restored to their rightful spots during a renovation in 1988.

PINBALL WIZARD

What's behind that secret door at the laundromat?

Sunshine Laundromat looks like any other laundromat in New York City. People carry in bags of dirty clothing, drop coins into the slot, and wait as the silver industrial machines get to work. But keep going, past the long line of washers and dryers, to the back of the laundromat where a secret door awaits. It's disguised to look like the door of a washing machine, but don't be afraid to pull it open. On the other side, a very different type of machine beckons.

In this room behind the laundromat, a collection of pinball machines lights up with fantastical colors. Players, whether they're waiting for their laundry to finish or just stopping by for fun, ardently tap the buttons on each side of the machines, hoping the flipper will keep their ball out of the gutter. Each machine offers

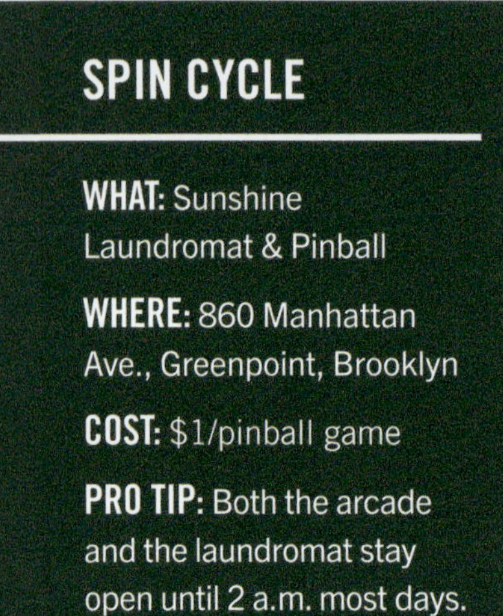

SPIN CYCLE

WHAT: Sunshine Laundromat & Pinball

WHERE: 860 Manhattan Ave., Greenpoint, Brooklyn

COST: $1/pinball game

PRO TIP: Both the arcade and the laundromat stay open until 2 a.m. most days.

Inside Sunshine Laundromat, there's a lot more to do than just washing and drying clothes.

Wash, dry, fold is a lot more exciting when you can reward yourself with a game of pinball after your chores.

a different theme, from 007 to Godzilla to Indiana Jones, all available to play for $1 per round. You'll need quarters to do so, but just like any good laundromat, there's of course a coin exchange machine.

In addition to the retro pinball machines, Sunshine also operates a bar in the back room with a long list of beers. If pinball isn't your game of choice, check out the tall tower of other board games available for visitors.

Rack up as many points as you can, but know it's going to be tough to get onto the leaderboard because pinball pros are known to frequent Sunshine.

ANY KITSCH WAY

Where do all of NYC's kitschiest items coexist?

A TEMPLE TO TCHOTCHKES

WHAT: City Reliquary museum

WHERE: 370 Metropolitan Ave., Williamsburg, Brooklyn

COST: $10, $8 for NYC residents

PRO TIP: The museum continues to grow its collection, so keep that in mind when you're cleaning out your closet.

Where can you find a collection of Statue of Liberty figurines, NYC World's Fair cups, a "very old hammer," and subway rail dust? A garbage dump, perhaps. But also the City Reliquary, a quirky museum in Brooklyn's Williamsburg neighborhood.

The museum, now housed on the ground floor of an apartment building, grew from a window display in founder Dave Herman's apartment window more than two decades ago. The tiny venue packs centuries of New York City into its two rooms. Artifacts fill display cases, cover the walls, and stretch onto the ceilings. While several other museums document the history of New York City, the City Reliquary is different because it tells the story of everyday New Yorkers, not the people making headlines. Its artifacts, partially sourced from residents of the city, help uncover lesser-known tales. They're the kinds of things your grandma might have kept in a china cabinet or tucked away in a cedar chest.

For example, a photo album on display documents kids' first haircuts. At Al Criscillo's Brooklyn barbershop, every kid got a portrait with their first haircut. The barber decorated his shop with the duplicate pictures. Now, those photos have found their way to the

The City Reliquary Museum strives to tell the story of everyday New Yorkers. The collection includes all manner of quirky items, which fill the museum from floor to ceiling.

City Reliquary, offering both a book full of sweet childhood moments and a look at fashion through the years. Other displays dig into the history of burlesque in the city and explore the city's love for seltzer.

While it's impossible to list all the gems crammed into this space, here are just a few more: a wooden block from the city's last remaining wooden sidewalk, a paint chip from the 6th Avenue L train platform, a pillowcase from the Plaza Hotel, core samples from Manhattan Island, a burned-out light bulb from the Statue of Liberty's torch, and several subway grab-holds.

The museum often hosts special rotating exhibits. Previous exhibitions have highlighted the famed Latin Quarter nightclub, NYC-themed tattoos, and NYC's "wonder women."

A FAN-TASTIC HOUSE

Why does that house on Joralemon Street look weird?

Amid the rows of three-story red brick homes along Joralemon Street in Brooklyn, there's one that doesn't quite fit in with the others. Its windows are blacked out. Its front door has an industrial handle, unlike the more attractive models next door. It doesn't have any decor; there's no wreath on the window, no window boxes, no doormat. It looks like an empty shell—and essentially, it is.

The MTA owns this house, also known as the Shaft House, and uses it as a fan plant and emergency exit for the subway. A remote-controlled ventilation system in the building helps circulate air through the subway tunnel. It can also quickly pull smoke out of the tunnel in case of a fire, a transit museum official explained.

The building dates back to 1847 when it was a private residence. But in the early 1900s, the Interborough Rapid Transit Company built a tunnel extending the subway from Manhattan to Brooklyn, and they needed a space for ventilation and emergency access. As they worked on the construction plans, there was one location that looked perfect for this industrial need: 58 Joralemon Street.

FROM HOUSE TO HELPER

WHAT: House turned subway vent

WHERE: 58 Joralemon St., Brooklyn Heights, Brooklyn

COST: Free

PRO TIP: The land in this area once belonged to Philip Livingston, a signer of the Declaration of Independence.

If you're a transit fan, also visit the New York Transit Museum. Located just a few blocks away, it's packed with fascinating artifacts about the city's subways—and even a fleet of boardable vintage subway cars.

Subway developers bought the property from a judge named Teunis Joralemon, dug beneath it, and reconfigured the home into a ventilation shaft house. Even to this day, their work still functions, offering extra peace of mind for train travelers.

While the general public can't go inside, transit officials assure there's nothing to see in there anyway. The house is filled with structural ironwork, and it emits a fan sound sometimes—that's it. But from the outside, this Greek Revival home presents a mystery for those willing to stop and look.

At first, this house may look like any other on Joralemon Street, but look closer to see why it doesn't quite match.The house dates back to 1847, but its use today is far different than it was back then.

A MOSAIC GROWS IN BROOKLYN

What's the story behind that mosaic house in Brooklyn?

The brick houses along Wyckoff Street in Brooklyn's Boerum Hill neighborhood boast plenty of traditional decorative features, like carved arches above the windows, ornate cornices, and colorfully painted doors. But one house takes architectural art to the next level.

A vibrant mosaic mural covers the first story of the yellow brick home at 108 Wyckoff. The artwork includes portrait silhouettes, an angel, an elephant, and several flowers. The words "Celebrate Life, Celebrate Love" wind through the scene. The artist, Susan Gardner, added those phrases after the September 11 terrorist attacks as "a way of communing with the grieving, trying to uplift us all."

PIECE BY PIECE

WHAT: Mosaic house

WHERE: 108 Wyckoff St., Boerum Hill, Brooklyn

COST: Free

PRO TIP: The artwork is in a residential neighborhood, so be respectful when visiting.

Traditional tile and glass make up some of the installation, but nontraditional materials like beads, buttons, and even CDs are put to use as well. The artwork stretches up toward the home's second floor. It overtakes the railing, patio floor, window boxes, and a bench, not just the brickwork.

Designed like an abstract Impressionist painting, the picture gets clearer farther away, while the artist's handiwork shines up close. Blue

---

With 50 years of painting experience, the artist says her work defies traditional molds and doesn't fit into one particular genre.

Tiny tiles and pieces of glass come together to create beautiful art in Brooklyn. This Wyckoff Street home stands out from the crowd.

and yellow tiles make up a girl's checkered dress, a variety of tan buttons combine to create a man's pants, and silver CDs add some colorful reflection to the scene.

Though the artwork is a treat to behold, it also shares important messages. One section spotlights civil rights martyrs, while another area focuses on climate change. As the artist wrote in a sign at the home, "I have made this statue of 'Mother Earth' holding 'The Future' on her lap—it is my plea for saner environmental practices which will determine if indeed 'Mother Earth' even has a future."

POWER TO THE PEOPLE

Who documents the social movements that shape the world?

Newspaper headlines may announce the news of a labor strike or a protest march, but who documents those stories for the long term? Their materials—flyers, zines, and T-shirts—may not make it into traditional museum or library collections, even though those stories are critical to our cultural understanding. That's where Interference Archive, a library and social center, comes in.

The Brooklyn-based organization documents the ephemera of social movements. Their collections include posters on the following topics, just to name a few: anarchy, anti-Capitalism, the Black Panther Party, disability rights, reproductive rights, LGBTQ issues, and environmentalism. These pieces are hard to find anywhere else.

Visitors are welcome to (carefully) browse through the open-stacks archival collection. That includes paging through drawers of large posters, pulling down boxes of zines, or even putting on a record. If you know

AN ACTIVIST ARCHIVE

WHAT: Interference Archive

WHERE: 314 7th St., Park Slope, Brooklyn

COST: Free

PRO TIP: The archive is powered by donations, so bring along some cash to support their work.

Head to this Park Slope address to browse zines, posters, and books. Visitors are welcome to touch these moments in history (gently!).

exactly what you're looking for, say posters by the Guerrilla Girls, the tidily organized subject list will help you locate it. But if you are just coming to browse, prepare to be awed by the creativity and passion in each item, from a short book titled *The Gay Liberation Movement* to a 1970s-era magazine called *Direct from Cuba.*

In addition to serving as a library, Interference Archive mounts special exhibitions highlighting items from the collection. Some recent exhibits have highlighted feminist struggles, police brutality, and public space in NYC.

In addition to regular open hours, look for special events like knitting meetups, educational reading groups, and listening parties.

A LOFTY APARTMENT

Is there really a secret apartment at Radio City Music Hall?

Tucked away from the world-renowned stage where the Radio City Rockettes perform kick after glorious kick, there's a quiet place for dining and entertaining. This secret apartment, known as the Roxy Suite, dates back to Radio City Music Hall's opening in the 1930s. With wood-paneled walls, gold-leaf ceilings, and Art Deco decor, the room feels like a time capsule from another era.

It once belonged to Samuel "Roxy" Rothafel, the impresario who spearheaded the opening of Radio City. The apartment is complete with a sitting area, a kitchen, and a dining room, which boasts a domed ceiling with incredible acoustics that enables all the guests around the table to hear one another, even when speaking at a whisper. There are conflicting stories as to whether Roxy actually lived in the apartment, which at one point included a bedroom, or just used it for entertaining.

However, one thing is for certain: the suite has been visited by many of the world's most famous stars, including Judy Garland, Walt Disney, and Alfred Hitchcock. That tradition continues today as VIP guests regularly visit the Roxy Suite. There's even a guestbook with some recognizable names of artists who have performed at Radio City, such as Olivia Rodrigo, Ali Wong, Harry Styles, Lady Gaga, Chris Rock, Oprah Winfrey, and many more.

On the Radio City Music Hall Tour Experience, you have the opportunity to walk through the suite and feel like a VIP yourself. Or if you really want the VIP experience, the room is available to rent for private events.

On the Radio City Music Hall Tour Experience, you'll also get to see the costume shop and even meet a Rockette!

"KICK" BACK

WHAT: Roxy Suite at Radio City, as part of the Radio City Music Hall Tour Experience

WHERE: 1260 Avenue of the Americas, Midtown, Manhattan

COST: $42 online or $33 at the box office.

MORE INFO: radiocity.com/tour

PRO TIP: Tours get very busy during the holiday season. If you can, try to book in the offseason.

This secret Art Deco apartment feels like stepping into the 1930s. Walk in the footsteps of some of the world's most famous recording artists who have also hung out here.

PEEP SHOW

Want to see a movie for free?

It's not usually advisable to stick your eye up close to a New York City wall, but it's worth making an exception at this charming site.

Head to the IFC Center in Greenwich Village, then glance to the right of the movie theater's marquee. Look closely and you'll find an unmarked silver metal circle with two quarter-size circles on the front. Those smaller circles are actually tiny covers that can be slid aside to reveal a miniature glass window. Gaze through, and you'll see whatever movie is playing inside the ground-level cinema. In addition to seeing the screen, you'll get a bird's-eye view into the theater itself.

The peepholes are intentionally hard to find, offering an Easter egg of sorts to reward the curious. Architect Larry Bogdanow added the peepholes when he transformed the Waverly Theatre into IFC Center in the early 2000s. During the renovation, staff wanted to find a way to make that smaller theater space more interesting. The late architect had an idea: peepholes. In addition to being funny and playful, the peephole draws on the design of old-school "Kinetoscopes" where people could pay a few cents to peer into a lens and see a film strip. Given that the IFC Center is the oldest continuously operating movie cinema in Manhattan, it's a fitting tribute to the industry's past.

PEEKABOO PICTURE

WHAT: The IFC Center peephole

WHERE: 323 6th Ave., Greenwich Village, Manhattan

COST: Free

PRO TIP: The peephole stands at about 5 feet, 5 inches tall, so shorter folks will need a boost to see.

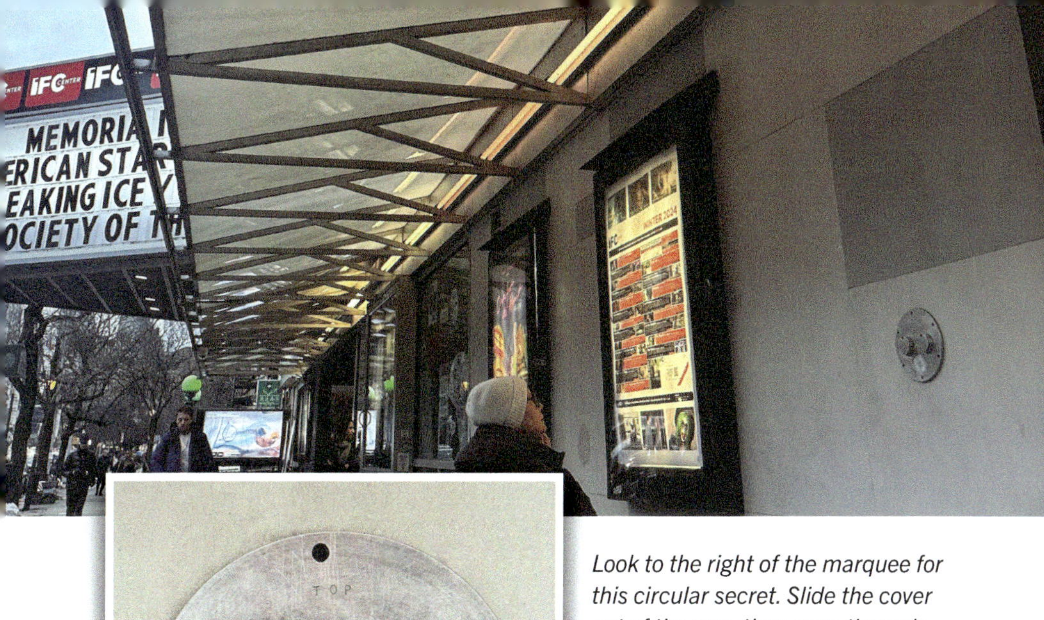

Look to the right of the marquee for this circular secret. Slide the cover out of the way, then gaze through for a very cool view.

The average passerby tends to breeze past these amusing openings, completely unaware of the cinematic scene that could unfold right before their eyes.

Sure, you could watch through the peephole, but go ahead and pay to watch the movie inside. The cinema specializes in independent films and hosts a variety of programming, including DOC NYC, America's largest documentary festival.

UNLOCKING A MYSTERY

What's the smallest freestanding building in Manhattan?

Measuring in at just 125 square feet, Greenwich Locksmiths squeezes tens of thousands of keys into a tiny triangular storefront. It's officially the smallest freestanding building with its very own lot and block number in Manhattan.

This slight storefront, however, holds a big history. The building dates back to 1921 when it was built as a tire shop, then became the offices of a fortune teller. Phil Mortillaro bought the property for his locksmith business back in 1980 for $20,000.

Since then, he's covered every inch of the shop's interior in keys and locks for sale. Meanwhile, the outside of the building is also covered in keys, but those ones are for artistic purposes. Over the course of a year, Mortillaro used about 10,000 keys to create a stunning mosaic partially inspired by Vincent van Gogh's *The Starry Night.* Neatly arranged spirals and lines of keys cascade across the storefront like fireworks. Some vintage skeleton keys even find their way into the pattern on the door.

With decades in the business, Mortillaro isn't ready to retire. He now works alongside his son, Phil Jr. Despite the store's small stature, the Mortillaros regularly hear overtures from people who want to buy it. A bank once offered $2 million. But Mortillaro won't budge.

It's important to note that this is the smallest freestanding building. That means there are other buildings that are technically smaller, but they're connected to other buildings. This one stands alone.

The beauty of this petite shop in Greenwich Village makes getting locked out of your apartment slightly less frustrating. Vincent van Gogh's The Starry Night *served as the inspiration for this mural created out of keys.*

MAJOR KEY

WHAT: Greenwich Locksmiths

WHERE: 56 7th Ave. S, Greenwich Village, Manhattan

COST: Free

PRO TIP: The store is open Monday through Friday.

He revels in the complexities of the locksmith business, from keys to safes to electronic security. As he told StreetEasy, "What am I going to do with the money? Isn't money supposed to make you happy? I'm already happy." Whatever the key to happiness is, this locksmith has found it.

A HIDDEN HOLOCAUST MEMORIAL

What's the message of this carved column at the courthouse?

On a building where justice is served, there's a powerful memorial to injustice. Titled *Memorial to All Victims of the Holocaust,* this column-size sculpture on a Manhattan courthouse includes an overhead view of Auschwitz 1 as seen on August 25, 1944. At the top left corner, there's a carving of the commandant's house; below it is a gas chamber and crematorium. Across the map, miniature sculptures represent an execution wall and torture chamber.

A statement in all caps wraps around the scene: "Indifference to injustice is the gate to Hell." Carved flames lap at the bottom of the carving and continue up the 38-foot-tall column. The column is meant to symbolize Auschwitz's chimney, which appeared to be part of a warehouse but actually disguised the gas chamber.

The chilling artwork, created in marble by Jewish artist Harriet Feigenbaum, reminds passersby of a deeply important message, exactly as court members intended. Aiming to make sure that the horrors of the Holocaust would never happen again, state court leaders invited artists to submit designs for a memorial at the courthouse. That was back in the 1980s; now more than 30 years later, surveys show a "shocking" lack of Holocaust knowledge among younger generations of Americans.

Find another Holocaust memorial in Riverside Park on the Upper West Side. The Warsaw Ghetto Memorial Plaza was installed in October 1947, making it one of the first Holocaust monuments in the United States.

The artist crafted the sculpture with Carrara marble, the same stone used to build the courthouse.

"INDIFFERENCE TO INJUSTICE IS THE GATE TO HELL"

WHAT: *Memorial to All Victims of the Holocaust*

WHERE: 27 Madison Ave., Flatiron District, Manhattan

COST: Free

PRO TIP: Also look up at the statues dotting the top of the courthouse.

To create the design, Feigenbaum studied photographs of death houses, along with a drawing made by a prisoner at Auschwitz. She also drew on an aerial photograph taken by the Allies. "By the selection of this photograph, the artist is saying that the Allies must have known of the camp and they took no action," according to the city's Department of Cultural Affairs. Notably, the artwork's flames and smoke appear to blow toward the courthouse, threatening the symbol of justice.

As the former NYC mayor Edward I. Koch said at the memorial's dedication ceremony in 1990, "The survivors of the concentration camps are now elderly and many are feeble. Soon they will be gone and no one will be left to recall personally what happened. This monument will serve as a remembrance."

EAT LIKE A FOUNDING FATHER

Where did the Founding Fathers hang out?

Days after the last British troops left American soil, President George Washington gathered his officers to thank them for their service and say goodbye before returning home.

The general is said to have shared this stirring line: "With a heart full of love and gratitude I now take leave of you. I most devoutly wish that your latter days may be as prosperous and happy as your former ones have been glorious and honorable."

The room where it happened, officially called the Long Room, still stands today at the Fraunces Tavern Museum. Staff preserved the room to look like an 18th-century public dining room. If you're wondering why these leaders met in a bar, that behavior was actually quite common in the Revolutionary era. At that time, taverns served as a center of civic and social life. The fledgling government even met and operated out of Fraunces Tavern before and after the American Revolution.

Washington's farewell address at the tavern happened on December 4, 1783, nine days after what's known as "Evacuation Day," aka the deadline for British troops and British loyalists to skedaddle. On that historic day—November 25, 1783—Washington rode his horse across Wall Street and down Broadway, leading his troops. He then went to Fraunces Tavern for a special dinner hosted by New York State Governor George Clinton. A few days later, he hosted his own noteworthy toast at the tavern.

A PATRIOTIC TOAST

WHAT: Fraunces Tavern Museum

WHERE: 54 Pearl St., Financial District, Manhattan

COST: $10 adults; $5 kids, students, and seniors

PRO TIP: In the tavern, order a pint and chicken pot pie—Washington's favorite.

Left: This brick building in Lower Manhattan is packed with history. Today, it's home to a museum and a restaurant. Right: This is called the Long Room. It's where George Washington delivered a powerful message to his troops in 1783.

Anybody can dine like an American rebel nowadays, as the Fraunces Tavern offers a dining room on the ground level. Upstairs, the Fraunces Tavern Museum dives into the history of the nation in a building older than the country itself.

While you're exploring Revolutionary history, also visit 39 Broadway where George Washington lived in 1790. The building, then called the McComb Mansion, no longer exists, but there's a plaque with a sketch of it.

A WEIRD WAX-TRAVAGANZA

Where can you find 1800s-era entertainment?

Entertainment looked a little different back in the late 1800s. One popular touring attraction called Castan's Panopticum featured wax figures, often grisly in appearance. These shows not only stoked Victorian-era titillation, they also served as helpful tools for medical research. They also made lots of money—up to 5,000 people would visit on a typical Sunday.

As photography and films came to prominence, these "shows of everything" became less popular. It just wasn't cool anymore to spend money and time at a wax museum when more exciting options were available. Given the waning interest, many wax collections didn't survive the early 1900s.

One collection, however, from the German Castan brothers stayed in storage in Europe. Decades later, a collector discovered the pieces and found a buyer for the whole lot: Tim League, CEO of the Alamo Drafthouse, a chain of movie theaters with vintage flair. The collection of creepy relics found a home inside the Alamo Drafthouse cinema in Downtown Brooklyn.

Dubbed House of Wax, the exhibition includes more than 100 anatomical models and 25 wax death masks (meaning a model of a dead person's face). There are death masks resembling Napoleon Bonaparte, Mary Queen of Scots, King Henry IV, and others, their eerily lifelike heads arranged on red velvet pillows as if sleeping.

The collection is a part of the cinema's bar and restaurant, which offers a variety of themed drinks. There's even a cognac-based drink called the Napoleon Death Mask.

Step right up to the House of Wax where you can see some Victorian-era entertainment. The collection includes more than 100 anatomical models and 25 wax death masks.

Other wax pieces depict birthmarks, the digestive system, birth, and more.

Red velvet curtains frame the entrance to the collection, along with a vintage sign lit up with incandescent bulbs. It feels as if a sideshow promoter could appear at any moment bellowing something like "Step right up! Finest collection of wax models here!"

WAXING POETIC

WHAT: House of Wax

WHERE: 445 Albee Sq. W, #4410, inside the City Point Building, Downtown Brooklyn

COST: Free

PRO TIP: While the collection is within a movie theater's lobby, you don't need a ticket to visit.

HEART OF STONE STREET

Where can you get a taste of old-world charm in Manhattan?

A CHARMING CORRIDOR

WHAT: Stone Street

WHERE: Stone St., between Coenties Alley and Hanover Square, Financial District, Manhattan

COST: Free

PRO TIP: Stone Street is divided into two sections on either side of the 85 Broad St. building, so be sure to find the cobblestoned pedestrian block at the cross streets listed above.

Steps away from the rushing traffic on Broadway, the whirring helicopters on the riverside helipad, and the chatter of tourists snapping photos at the Charging Bull statue sits a peaceful pathway known as Stone Street. This pedestrian-friendly roadway in Lower Manhattan transports visitors to Europe with its cobblestone pathways and string lights.

Though it's a popular spot for locals and visitors, the street's history tends to get overlooked. Stone Street was the first paved road in New York City—and it's one of the oldest streets in the city. One section of the road was first called High Street and another section was named Breuers Straet, then later Brouwer Straat (aka Brewer Street) because several breweries were located there in the 1650s. One tale says that residents pooled their money to pave the street with cobblestones as way to make beer deliveries easier.

When the British took over, they changed the name to Stony Street, and it eventually became Stone Street. Because of the Great Fire of 1835, the original buildings disappeared, but many of the rebuilt structures have remained unchanged since then. Stepping inside the cozy Stone Street Tavern or Ulysses' Folkhouse, for example, feels like a jaunt back in time.

Walk along this cobblestone street to get a sense of New York City in an earlier era.

While the street seems serene most of the time, it becomes a busy scene on weekends and for special events, like Oktoberfest and St. Patrick's Day. The celebrations spill out of the bars and restaurants and onto the streets. In a way, they're paying tribute to those Dutch brewers from centuries before.

Packed with restaurants and bars, Stone Street offers cuisine for every palate. There's an Irish pub, a Spanish tapas bar, a Cuban restaurant, a natural wine bar, and lots more.

A MARILYN MOMENT

Where was the iconic Marilyn Monroe dress scene filmed?

"Ooh do you feel the breeze from the subway? Isn't it delicious?!" Marilyn Monroe gleefully chirps in the iconic scene from *The Seven Year Itch.* She utters that line while standing atop a Manhattan subway grate as a train rumbles below, sending the skirt of her pleated white dress billowing into the air around her. The camera pans to her bare legs, white heels, and red toenails—extremely racy for 1955.

The scene was technically filmed in New York City at 52nd Street and Lexington, where you can go take your very own Marilyn photo. But no matter how long you stand there waiting for a train to blow air through the subway grates, it's not going to happen. You will definitely hear trains whiz beneath the ground, but that's about it. To create the windy effect, crews installed a fan beneath the grate.

The subway grates still exist in the same spot. It's hard to tell exactly which one Marilyn stood on, but it looks to be about the fifth grate on Lexington based on movie stills and clips. Those clips, though, can't necessarily be trusted. That original footage in Manhattan was ditched and replaced with footage staged in Hollywood. There are several reasons why crews discarded the NYC footage. First, men were heard brashly catcalling in the background "Higher! Higher!" as her dress lifted. Monroe's then-husband, Joe DiMaggio, was also in the crowd, and he didn't like the risqué scene (they divorced just a few weeks later). Monroe may have wanted to redo the scene to calm him. Finally, it's possible that the scene was a publicity stunt all along.

That beautiful white dress with its pleated skirt sold at auction in 2011 for more than $5.5 million. Just go take a Marilyn-style picture instead for free.

Have your "Marilyn moment" at these grates—though don't expect that your clothing will actually blow in the breeze. The site's not marked, and it looks just like any other grate, making this a true secret.

Though the final footage was still provocative for the era, it was toned down significantly from the original version filmed in New York City. The ubiquitous photos of Marilyn in her dress are from that original NYC scene where the dress floats around her.

A DARING DRESS ADDRESS

WHAT: Filming location of Marilyn Monroe's iconic dress scene

WHERE: 590 Lexington Ave., at the intersection of East 52nd St., Midtown East, Manhattan

COST: Free

PRO TIP: There's no marker or plaque indicating this iconic grate, making it a true secret.

"AIN'T AFRAID OF NO GHOSTS"

"DON'T CROSS THE STREAMS"

WHAT: *Ghostbusters* firehouse

WHERE: 14 N Moore St., Tribeca, Manhattan

COST: Free

PRO TIP: It's an active fire station, so be mindful of the firefighters at work.

Who ya gonna call?

When the Ectomobile peels out of its headquarters ready to take on its latest mission, it's actually departing a real, working fire department. Officially called Hook & Ladder Company 8, its neighborhood might look gritty in the 1980s hit movie *Ghostbusters,* but it's really located in what's now one of the fanciest neighborhoods in the city.

Fans of the film can visit the three-story station in Tribeca, though they're limited to visiting the exterior, which is the only part actually shown in the movie anyway. Forget sliding down the fire pole like Dr. Peter Venkman. In the movie, a shabby sign reading "Ghostbusters" is tacked above the arched garage door; in real life, you'll see a carved sign with the fire company's name in that spot. The sign will tell you if you're in the right place, but you'll likely first spot the illuminated *Ghostbusters* logo, which perches on the front of the building.

While you're there, look up at the skyline to see what's colloquially called the "Jenga Building." This incredible tower at 56 Leonard Street seems to defy gravity with its cantilevered design.

Scenes in Ghostbusters *were filmed at this actual fire station in Tribeca.The fire station leans into its pop culture fame with references to the movie.*

Even though it's a working fire station, it's clear that the firefighters have some fun with the building's history. On the sidewalk outside of the station, there are two painted illustrations, both with comic book-style renderings of a ghost holding fire equipment. One of the ghosts even wears a Ladder 8 fire helmet. With depictions of fire ladders and fire hydrants, the artwork pulls together the building's purpose with its cinematic history.

If you visit during the daytime when the fire station is open and the firefighters aren't too busy, you can occasionally step inside the lobby to get a peek at the building and even purchase souvenirs with the fire company's logo.

Other *Ghostbusters* filming locations include Rockefeller Center, Columbia University, New York Public Library, and Lincoln Center.

AN EXTREMELY HIP HISTORY

Where was hip-hop born?

Imagine this: it's August 1973, and you get an invitation to a back-to-school party. The invitation, written in black ballpoint pen on a classic lined note card, calls it "A DJ Kool Herc Party: Back to School Jam." It's taking place at 1520 Sedgwick Ave. in a Bronx apartment building's rec room from 9 p.m. to 4 a.m. It only costs 25 cents for ladies and 50 cents for "fellas" to get in.

"TO THE HIP, HIP-HOP AND YOU DON'T STOP THE ROCKIN'"

WHAT: Birthplace of hip-hop

WHERE: 1520 Sedgwick Ave., Morris Heights, Bronx

COST: Free

PRO TIP: Look for the street sign declaring Sedgwick Avenue as "Hip Hop Boulevard."

That back-to-school get-together turned out to be one of the most pivotal moments in music history. That night, hip-hop was born, kicking off a revolutionary music style that was percolating in New York City and soon took over the airwaves.

Clive Campbell, known as Hercules or Kool Herc because of his height, grew up in Jamaica, and he was deeply influenced by his home country's musical traditions. He remembered Jamaican dance halls where DJs gave toasts during their performances. Plus, in New York, he noticed how partygoers liked the exciting percussive "break" in the music, so he set up two

---

Not far from 1520 Sedgwick, work is underway on the Universal Hip Hop Museum, which will celebrate the genre's roots in the Bronx and its evolution.

Just a street sign marks the Bronx apartment building where hip-hop was born. Sedgwick Avenue is now nicknamed Hip Hop Boulevard.

turntables to elongate the break. His friend Coke La Rock began rapping. Suddenly, those components came together for a completely new style of music.

Fellow DJs Afrika Bambaataa and Grandmaster Flash are credited along with Herc for creating the foundations and culture of the genre. In addition to DJing and emceeing, hip-hop also consists of breakdancing, style writing (graffiti), and knowledge. All of those elements were born in the Bronx, and hip-hop soon spread across the other four boroughs—and the world.

THE TALE OF THE MOVING STATUE

Why does that statue along East Drive keep moving?

It's only fitting that a tribute to a marathon runner ought to stay on the move. On most days of the year, runners jog past a statue of a man in sneakers, a tracksuit, and a ball cap standing on the eastern side of Central Park, attentively looking at his wristwatch. But on the first Sunday in November, the statue disappears, moving westward to the finish line of the New York City Marathon.

The statue depicts Fred Lebow, who cofounded the New York City Marathon in 1970. Back then, the race through Central Park welcomed 127 entrants, 55 of whom finished the course. He used his own money to buy prizes for the first people across the finish line. Over the years, the city's marathon has grown into one of the most renowned races in the world, welcoming more than 50,000 runners for a challenging race that spans the five boroughs.

Lebow, a longtime president of the New York Road Runners Club, grew up in Romania in an Orthodox Jewish family. In his youth, he escaped the Nazis and the Communists and eventually moved to America. With a passion for running, he got involved with the Road Runners club, helping to build on the legacy established by remarkable Black athletes and coaches Joe Yancey Jr. and Ted Corbitt. They all shared the same ethos: the race must be open to all races, genders, and abilities.

Athletes have been known to touch the statue for good luck and sometimes even leave flowers by his running shoes, especially on marathon day.

Fellow runner Daniel Mitrovich wanted to honor Lebow's legacy and vision, so he spearheaded an effort to have a statue made to stand in Central Park. The sculpture, created by artist Jesus Ygnacio Dominguez, was unveiled in 1994, shortly after Lebow's death from cancer.

Now, the statue stands along a popular exercise trail, offering a coach's encouragement to all who walk, jog, or run by.

A STATUE WITH SOLES AND SOUL

WHAT: *Fred Lebow statue*

WHERE: 90th Street and East Drive in Central Park, Upper East Side, Manhattan (except on New York Marathon day)

COST: Free

PRO TIP: The statue is located along a busy path, so keep alert for runners who may blow past.

Look for this statue of Fred Lebow at 90th Street and East Drive in Central Park. The statue is aptly placed along a jogging path.

PIPE DREAMS

What does a Muppeteer do when they get bored?

There's not much to do while waiting in a backstage dressing room for hours. Jim Henson and the rest of the team behind the Muppets discovered that pretty quickly as they waited for their appearance on the Jack Paar television show in 1964.

Inside a utility closet at NBC's famed 30 Rock building, they noticed some pipes and decided to keep themselves entertained by decorating them. After all, if anybody had the ability to bring boring gray pipes to life, this was the right crew for the job. They decorated each one with silly faces, some with mops of hair, others with teeth showing, and some with glasses. They cleverly used the pipes' features to enhance their artwork, like making disc-shaped segments appear as mouths or hats. The puppeteers used a variety of colors in their work, making characters with green, yellow, and red faces.

A MUPPET MYSTERY

WHAT: Muppet Pipes

WHERE: 30 Rockefeller Plz., Midtown, Manhattan

COST: $48 adults; $42 kids, seniors, and military

PRO TIP: Photos and videos aren't allowed on the tour, so be sure to take some mental snapshots.

The Tour at NBC Studios also goes behind the scenes of some of the studios where shows like *SNL, The Tonight Show Starring Jimmy Fallon,* and more are produced and taped. Plus, the tour showcases the fascinating history of TV from the building where history is made over and over again.

You can only see the Muppet Pipes on the Tour at NBC Studios, and photos aren't allowed or shared publicly, so you've got to see it to believe it.

They even signed their work, painting in yellow "With love from the Muppets" at the bottom of the pipes.

Their artwork was hidden away behind Studio 6B for years, but now the Muppet Pipes are available for all to see on the Tour at NBC Studios.

A MASTERPIECE FOR THE ORIGINAL MUCKRAKER

What are all those big bronze heads on Roosevelt Island?

After growing up in rural Pennsylvania in the late 1800s, Nellie Bly (officially Elizabeth Jane Cochran) made a name for herself as a newspaper journalist. In response to a sexist article decrying working women, Bly wrote a letter to the editor titled "The Girl Puzzle." Her writing advocated for poor working women and explained the social advantages afforded to boys, not girls. Intrigued by her comments, the editor offered her a job at the *Pittsburgh Dispatch.* After two years at the newspaper, she headed to work in New York City, leaving with the note: "I'm off for New York. Look out for me. Bly"

In New York, her first assignment at Joseph Pulitzer's *New York World Newspaper* was to investigate the Blackwell's Island Asylum by getting committed and reporting undercover. She succeeded and wrote gut-wrenching stories about the women there who experienced horrific treatment. Her pioneering journalism led to significant reforms at the facility.

A powerful monument on Roosevelt Island now stands near the site of the former mental health facility. Titled *The Girl Puzzle,* the artwork features large-scale renderings of women's faces meant to symbolize real women who have endured and overcome hardship. Next to a sculpture of Nellie Bly's face, other faces represent Asian,

---

Nellie Bly's career also included working as a World War I correspondent, an inventor, and a suffragist. She even set the world record for circumnavigation of the earth in 72 days.

The Girl Puzzle *monument stands on Roosevelt Island. This powerful artwork pays homage to journalist and adventurer Nellie Bly.*

Black, immigrant, queer, young, and old women. Their faces appear partially broken and repaired, like puzzle pieces. Mirrored spheres encourage visitors to interact with the artwork and see how fragments come together at different points. The monument was designed by Amanda Matthews of Prometheus Art. Quotes from Bly, such as "While I live I hope" are posted around the monument.

Known as America's first investigative journalist, Nellie Bly gave a voice to women, children, and workers—anyone without visibility. As she said, "I have never had but one desire, and that was to benefit humanity."

THE "WOMEN'S SPHERE"

WHAT: *The Girl Puzzle* monument

WHERE: Northern tip of Roosevelt Island, Manhattan

COST: Free

PRO TIP: Also walk over to the Octagon, which was once part of the New York City Lunatic Asylum.

A LEGACY OF SELF-DETERMINATION AND FREEDOM

How did this section of Brooklyn become a powerful free Black community in pre-Civil War America?

When New York abolished slavery in 1827, the legislation didn't automatically grant Black residents full citizenship. Instead, the state's constitution said that Black men must own $250 worth of property to be eligible to vote. In response, a dockworker named James Weeks joined with other African American investors to buy property and create a self-governing community they called Weeksville.

Weeks took out ads in prominent Black newspapers encouraging people to move to Weeksville for a new life. The ads worked, attracting settlers from the region, the South, the Caribbean, and Africa. Weeksville became one of the largest free Black communities in pre-Civil War America.

Many people took refuge at Weeksville after the Civil War draft riots in 1863, during which Black Americans faced severe racial violence in Lower Manhattan that killed hundreds and drove thousands from their homes. They saw Weeksville as accessible but far removed from the danger in Manhattan. At its peak in the 1870s to 1880s, Weeksville numbered about 500 people across 100 houses. The community grew and thrived with a variety of Black institutions, such as a home for seniors, an orphanage, and

---

During its heyday, Weeksville's hub was around present-day Troy Avenue and Dean Street, located a few blocks from the heritage center.

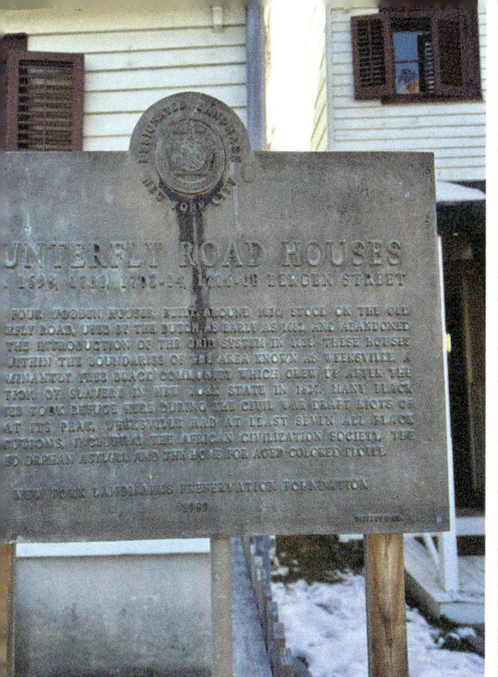

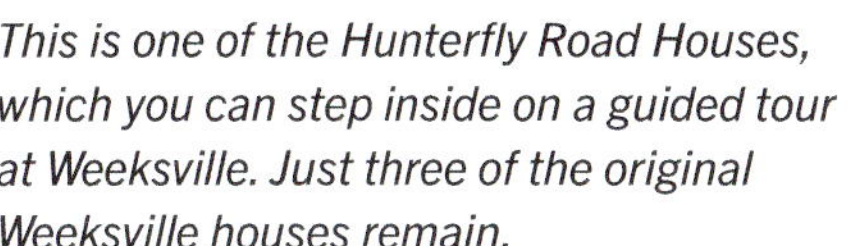

This is one of the Hunterfly Road Houses, which you can step inside on a guided tour at Weeksville. Just three of the original Weeksville houses remain.

WANDERING THROUGH WEEKSVILLE

WHAT: Weeksville Heritage Center

WHERE: 158 Buffalo Ave., Crown Heights, Brooklyn

COST: Free to visit; guided tours are $8

PRO TIP: Though the grounds are free to visit, you'll need to book a tour to go inside the homes.

a chapter of the African Civilization Society. Families in Weeksville benefited from the empowerment of owning private property as well as having a community of neighbors in close proximity.

In the 1960s, however, plans emerged to demolish Weeksville to build public housing. Community leaders were able to save a few of Weeksville's homes, and the Weeksville Heritage Center continues to preserve the history of the area amid rapid gentrification.

Today, three of those original houses remain. Called the Historic Hunterfly Road Houses, one represents the 1860s, another the 1900s, and a third the 1930s. The homes haven't been moved or rebuilt, allowing visitors to walk in the footsteps of the people who lived there.

AN INK-SPIRED ADVENTURE

Where can you try your hand at an 1800s-era craft?

Back in the 1800s, printing a document wasn't as easy as clicking file > print. Instead, this process involved special tools called wooden types, messy ink, and plenty of oomph to operate the large machinery by hand. Despite the challenges, printers endured because their important work helped to power New York City's booming economy. As traders arrived on ships, they needed stationery, invoices, and ads, and that put a big demand on printers. By 1900, the city was home to more than 700 printing offices, many in the historic Seaport District, given its proximity to the water.

Nowadays, you can experience the old-school letterpress printing process at South Street Seaport Museum's Bowne & Co. Stationers. The original Bowne & Co. dates back to 1775 when it was founded as a small offering of dry goods and stationery, and later became a successful job-printing business, specializing in documents for the expanding banking industry.

PRESS HERE

WHAT: Bowne & Co. Stationers

WHERE: 211 Water St., Seaport, Manhattan

COST: Free

PRO TIP: Even though the workshops are free, be sure to reserve your spot in advance online.

To continue nerding out over fascinating history in the Seaport, continue through the rest of the South Street Seaport Museum where you can learn about the city's maritime history through art, artifacts, and a fleet of historic vessels.

On a visit to Bowne & Co. you'll see historic printing equipment like this machine. Sign up for a workshop where you'll get to try out these old machines and make some cards to take home.

Today, the stationery shop sells a variety of wares, such as candles, oddities, and home decor, plus a wide array of printed and paper goods. In addition to perusing the paper creations made by pro printers, you can make your own at special workshops. During the monthly Fresh Prints workshop, for example, see printing equipment from a variety of eras, then try it out and take home your creation. The shop often hosts seasonal workshops, too, where you can make cards for Valentine's Day or Mother's Day.

CHECK OUT THIS CHECKMATE

Why is that chessboard so big?

It's not uncommon to see chess matches in parks across the city, especially at Union Square. Determined competitors bend their necks over their boards to focus on their next move. Their intense games even draw crowds of onlookers. While the games played on those chessboards may be full of big drama, the pieces themselves are typically miniature.

Over in Midtown East, though, the chess pieces balloon in size. *Giant Chess,* a 1982 installation on the side of a red brick apartment building, takes the game to soaring new heights. This vertically mounted gigantic game takes over three stories; each chess piece measures in at 2.5 feet. A plaque at the site calls it the "World's Largest Chessboard," but several other chessboards around the world also claim that title. Whether or not it's the biggest, though, doesn't matter. It's a delightful diversion in the middle of Manhattan.

The artwork is a credit to Melvyn and Robert Kaufman, brothers who led a major real estate company and were known for creative designs. When they built the office tower at 767 3rd Avenue, they wanted to gussy up the bland wall that overlooked their skyscraper's public plaza.

Just a few steps up 3rd Avenue, stop by 777 3rd Avenue to see Big Red Swing, another piece of public art commissioned by the Kaufmans.

PAWN STOP

WHAT: *Giant Chess*

WHERE: 212 E 48th St., Midtown East, Manhattan

COST: Free

PRO TIP: Though the artwork's address is technically 767 3rd Avenue, you'll find it on the 48th Street side of the buildling.

Giant Chess *was installed in 1982 in Midtown East. Each chess piece soars to a height taller than 2 feet.*

In past years, a cherry picker used to move one oversize piece each week to depict famous historical chess matches, but the pieces haven't moved in a while based on recent observations. Even so, the behemoth board is a sight to behold.

A variety of benches and tables sit beneath the chessboard, each one big enough to support lunch—or a game of chess.

BURIED HISTORY

What was on the west side of Manhattan before Central Park?

The popular playgrounds, trails, and theaters along Central Park's west side were built atop historic land with an important and recently unearthed backstory. The park's footprint between West 82nd and West 89th Streets was once home to Seneca Village, a thriving community inhabited mostly by African Americans, along with a few Irish and German immigrants.

With about 225 residents as of 1855, the neighborhood was one of the few African American enclaves at that time. Seneca Village offered residents a respite from the unhealthy conditions and racial discrimination in downtown Manhattan. The community constructed churches, harvested gardens, and built homes. Notably, many Black residents owned their homes, which provided them the right to vote.

In the early 1850s, city planners decided to build a large park, and Seneca Village stood within the borders they'd outlined. With eminent domain laws on their side, the city forced all landowners within the park to leave by 1857, then razed the buildings. Some of the buildings in Seneca Village had stood there since 1825. Though landowners across the park were compensated, some protested the assessments, claiming their property was undervalued.

While this history was literally buried for more than a century, archaeologists conducted excavations on the site in 2011. They found artifacts including an iron tea kettle, a roasting pan, a stoneware beer bottle, and a small shoe, all items that help tell the story of what daily life was like in Seneca Village.

REMEMBERING SENECA VILLAGE

WHAT: Seneca Village

WHERE: Central Park between West 82nd and West 89th Streets, Upper West Side, Manhattan

COST: Free

PRO TIP: The park often offers in-depth tours of this area; check the park's website to register.

In the early 1800s, Seneca Village was a thriving African American enclave. On the west side of Central Park, look for signs indicating notable sites in this lost neighborhood.

These days, this area looks like the rest of the park with its rolling hills, massive boulders, and leafy trees. Recently, the Central Park Conservancy installed 16 signs that tell the story of this important community. The signs, for example, mark sites where the African Union Church once stood and where the Reservoir Keepers used to live—each one a reminder of this shattered history.

For a self-guided tour of Seneca Village, enter at Central Park West and West 85th Street. To make sure you find all 16 signs, pick up a brochure at any park visitors' center or download a map online.

COKE THAT CAUSES A STIR

Where can you sip a retro refreshment?

For more than a century, Lexington Candy Shop has been serving the classics, like egg creams, BLTs, and omelets. They do it all the old-school way—by hand with precision honed over the decades. They even make their Coke the old-fashioned way. Instead of serving the popular drink from a fountain soda machine or from cans, they whip it up from scratch, a rare treat that's hard to find anywhere else.

The recipe itself isn't a secret. If you get a seat at the counter, you can watch the busy staff make it happen. First, they fill a glass with ice then squeeze in a few pumps of Coke syrup. Next they pull down the handle of an old-school seltzer machine to add liquid and carbonation. All the while, they use a long metal spoon to vigorously mix the beverage. The finished product offers the drink's original taste, which is a bit different than the soda we're used to today. It's less fizzy than a typical fountain Coke, and the taste feels a bit smoother. But it's just as delicious and pairs perfectly with lunch at this time-capsule restaurant. Coke floats are also on the menu for an extra-decadent refreshment.

DON'T BURST MY BUBBLE

WHAT: Lexington Candy Shop

WHERE: 1226 Lexington Ave., Upper East Side, Manhattan

COST: A small Coke costs $3.65

PRO TIP: The line on the weekend can be long. To beat the crowd, visit on a weekday.

The restaurant's name, Lexington Candy Shop, harkens back to the days when it sold homemade candy in addition to serving up breakfast and lunch.

The luncheonette serves a large array of diner classics, drawing long lines on the weekends. Inside, not much has changed over the years. The worn counter bears imprints from years of hard work, a vintage milkshake machine whirs away, and a labyrinth of booths fill up with hungry New Yorkers.

Family-owned for more than a century, the restaurant was founded in 1925 by Soterios Philis and Tami Naskos then passed down to Philis's son Peter, and then his son John, along with business partner Bob Karcher.

Find Lexington Candy Shop on the Upper East Side—and be prepared to wait for a table on the weekends. This Coke is way better than what you can get in a can.

FOR THE BIRDS

Why are there subtropical birds in this Brooklyn cemetery?

Since 1863, a soaring Gothic arch has welcomed visitors to The Green-Wood Cemetery, a famed final resting place in Brooklyn. But now that arch is home to some very chirpy greeters: a flock of green and gray monk parakeets.

The colorful birds, which are a type of parrot that originates in South America, surprisingly arrived at Green-Wood during the late 1970s or early 1980s. Nobody knows exactly how they got here, but there are rumors, explains Sara Evans, director of living collections and curator at The Green-Wood Cemetery. The birds could have escaped from a shipment of monk parakeets at the airport or an international shipping terminal. It's also possible that the flock started from a few pet birds that escaped or were released. Either way, around 35 to 40 monk parakeets now call Green-Wood's Gothic arch home.

After straggling out of their nest in the morning, the birds feed on seeds and herbaceous material. Once full, they turn their attention to daily upkeep on their complex nest, which Evans says is almost like an apartment building. They forage for tiny twigs then meticulously build and rearrange the sticks until they're satisfied. They also spend

"CHEEP" FUN

WHAT: The Green-Wood Cemetery monk parakeets

WHERE: 500 25th St., Greenwood Heights, Brooklyn

COST: Free

PRO TIP: Enter the main entrance at 5th Avenue and 25th Street, which is open daily.

The birds are active throughout the day, especially in the morning and late afternoon just before sunset, so you're likely to see them any day that you visit.

About 35 to 40 monk parakeets call Green-Wood's Gothic arch home. The birds spend time preening and snuggling, making for adorable photos. Photo courtesy of Evan Rabeck.

time preening and snuggling each other, which makes for some extremely cute photos. As the day comes to a close, the parakeets perch on their nest and watch the sunset together until bedtime. Though they hail from warmer climates, the adaptable avians can live happily in New York, especially thanks to their cozy nest.

The cemetery staff doesn't bother them, and they don't bother the cemetery staff. In fact, they may have found the perfect location for their nest. There's basically no human contact, and the arch is a protected landmark, so it'll stay there forever. The mysterious birds have become a de facto mascot for Green-Wood, delighting visitors with their sounds and squawks.

DEEP ROOTS

What's the oldest living thing in NYC?

As cars roar by on the Long Island Expressway, a dense forest of trees next to the highway generously endures the pollution and clears the air day after day. One tree there, dubbed the Alley Pond Giant, stands the test of time. Dating back to the 1600s, this tulip tree is thought to be the oldest and tallest living organism in New York City.

The tree is perhaps the last remaining witness to the city's evolution. It was there when the Indigenous Matinecock people walked through the forest and when Dutch settlers arrived in the city. To put it into perspective, the tree is so old that it would have been a well-established young tree when George Washington passed the area on a tour of Long Island in 1790.

When measured in 2000, the tree soared to a height of 133.8 feet with a girth of 18.6 feet. The Alley Pond Giant, also known as the Queens Giant Tulip Tree, lives in Alley Pond Park. Visiting the tree can be a little tricky. There's a trail entrance along East Hampton Boulevard near the intersection with the Horace Harding Expressway. On East Hampton Boulevard, look for the sign along the fence about the Alley Pond Giant. Enter the trail there, and you'll see a dense cluster of trees on your left. The Alley Pond Giant stands among them, protected by a fence and nestled deep into the forest. It would be a pretty treacherous hike to get close to the tree, so stay on the trail and admire it from afar.

A TOWERING TREE

WHAT: The Alley Pond Giant

WHERE: Inside Alley Pond Park, Bayside, Queens

COST: Free

PRO TIP: Enter on the trail at the intersection of East Hampton Boulevard and Horace Harding Expressway.

This stand of trees in Bayside, Queens isn't just a pretty sight—it's also home to the city's oldest living organism in the city. Just steps from this historic tree, cars roar by on the Long Island Expressway.

Though the Alley Pond Giant is well over three centuries old, tulip trees are known to live up to 600 years and grow to more than 150 feet, meaning this towering tree still has room to grow and continue cleaning the air for us, as long as we continue to protect it.

A TRIP DOWN MEMORY LANE

Can you go back in time to your childhood?

The nostalgia comes in waves at dAN's Parents' House, a charming vintage shop on an oft-overlooked island, where 500,000 items fill floor to ceiling. Trinkets and tchotchkes pack every inch inside this pastel green and pink Victorian building that husband-and-wife team Dan Treiber and Reina Mia Brill saved from demolition and transformed into a haven for misfit toys and vintage ephemera.

In the front room alone, shoppers can peruse collections of Troll dolls, Rubik's Cubes, skeleton keys, license plates, My Little Pony toys, and so much more. A wooden bureau functions like a cabinet of curiosities, with drawers dedicated to action figures, sand timers, watches, magnets, cassettes, vintage cards, and 1960s dime-store items. It's not uncommon to hear visitors joyfully exclaim, "I had that toy!" or "I remember that!" when they discover forgotten items from their childhood, from ViewMasters to die-cast cars.

The business began in 2009 when the couple wanted to buy Treiber's childhood home but didn't have the funding. A friend suggested that they try setting up a booth at a local flea market to sell Treiber's childhood toys that still packed his parents' house. The booth quickly became a hit with its wide array of collectibles, and they eventually expanded to the building at 239 City Island Ave., not far from where Treiber grew up.

The store's record room recently underwent a massive renovation, and it offers several bins of vinyl from the Beatles to Springsteen to Vangelis, plus a collection of old-school concert backstage passes.

This pastel Victorian home serves as a haven for misfit toys and vintage ephemera. Spend time perusing the shelves, bins, and cabinets packed with toys and tchotchkes.

WORK HARD, PLAY HARD

WHAT: dAN's Parents' House

WHERE: 239 City Island Ave., City Island, Bronx

COST: Free to visit

PRO TIP: Check the shop's website and Instagram (@dansparentshouse) for hours of operation; standard hours are Wednesday–Sunday 11am to 7pm with expanded hours in the summer and weekends only in January and February.

In addition to sourcing and selling treasured memorabilia, the couple became boosters for City Island, the section of the Bronx they call home. Brill fondly calls it "the mythical island in the Bronx." On the narrow island, you're never too far from the water. Boats, seafood restaurants, and quaint shops line its main street giving a beach-town vibe. If it weren't for the Manhattan skyline in the distance, you'd hardly know you were in New York City at all.

A BRIGHT IDEA

Are there any lighthouses left in Manhattan?

The rocky shoreline in the Jeffrey's Hook area of the Hudson River wreaked havoc on ship after ship in the 1800s. To help sailors navigate this treacherous area on the northwestern end of Manhattan, officials installed a pole with candle-powered lanterns. When barge captains eventually demanded a brighter beacon, there was a relatively simple solution: a recently dismantled lighthouse that once stood in New Jersey but had been rendered obsolete there.

After that New Jersey lighthouse was dismantled, the Coast Guard reassembled it in New York City in 1921, calling this red lighthouse the Jeffrey's Hook Lighthouse. Its blinking lamp and fog bell helped to guide sailors through the tricky waters. But after just a decade, the lighthouse was once again rendered obsolete. This time, it was because the George Washington Bridge opened directly above it, bathing the area in light.

The Coast Guard planned to demolish the lighthouse, much to the dismay of New Yorkers who had grown

ILLUMINATING THE LAST LIGHTHOUSE IN MANHATTAN

WHAT: The Little Red Lighthouse

WHERE: Fort Washington Park along the Hudson River Greenway beneath the George Washington Bridge, Washington Heights, Manhattan

COST: Free

PRO TIP: For tours of the lighthouse's interior, call the Urban Park Rangers at 212-360-2774 or visit nyc.gov/parks.

Lighthouses have different patterns of lights to help boaters recognize them from afar. The Little Red Lighthouse, for example, flashes one second of light followed by two seconds of darkness.

Nobody ever lived in the lighthouse but a part-time attendant ran the light.

accustomed to the charming attraction. Thanks to the public outcry and even a children's book called *The Little Red Lighthouse and the Great Gray Bridge,* the lighthouse was saved and eventually given to NYC Parks.

As the last surviving lighthouse in Manhattan, the site draws joggers, bikers, and tourists to its spot along the coastline in Fort Washington Park. Find it directly beneath the George Washington Bridge in Manhattan; as cars whiz by above, the lighthouse harkens back to a simpler time. Today, the lighthouse stands as a reminder of the city's maritime past and the importance of allowing everybody's light to shine.

AN ARCH-ITECTURAL MARVEL

What's that old arch doing in Inwood?

Wedged among an auto body shop, a car lot, a grocery store, and brick apartment complexes near the 1 train line in Inwood, there's an architectural feature that doesn't quite fit in: a soaring marble archway. Though it's now missing several chunks and is covered in graffiti, its wear and tear can't belie the archway's grand design.

This 35-foot-tall, 20-foot-deep archway was the entrance to an estate built in 1855 by the Seaman family. Over the years, the property changed hands, and the land eventually became an apartment development. The only piece that remains is the arch.

In its earlier days, the arch must have been a sight to behold. Designed after the Arc de Triomphe in Paris, the Inwood arch boasted ornate carved brackets and two spaces for statuary. A smattering of windows along the back of the arch likely were part of a gatekeeper's quarters. The arch was so extravagant that locals called it "Seaman's folly."

In 1905, a man named Thomas Dwyer bought the estate. Even if you don't know his name, you've definitely seen his buildings. Dwyer worked as a contractor who helped to build the Soldiers' and Sailors' Monument and the Metropolitan Museum of Art, and he turned the arch into an office space. Eventually, he sold the property to a developer who built an apartment complex, but the arch still stands.

SEAMAN'S FOLLY STILL STANDS

WHAT: Seaman-Drake Arch

WHERE: Broadway at W 216th St., Inwood, Manhattan

COST: Free

PRO TIP: The arch is located just steps from the 215th Street subway station. You can even see it from the subway window if you look closely.

Once a grand entrance, the Seaman-Drake Arch now is a mostly forgotten relic squeezed between an apartment building and an auto shop. You can even catch a glimpse of it from the 215th Street subway station.

These days, it curves atop an auto body repair shop, framing the work taking place beneath its crumbling marble facade.

There was talk in the early 2000s about turning the archway complex into a nightclub, but that never materialized. Instead, the arch stands in Inwood as it has for more than a century.

A GROWING SECRET IN MIDTOWN

Where can you find greenery amid the concrete jungle?

Midtown Manhattan isn't known for its greenery. But a secret garden grows amid the blocks of gray skyscrapers—you just have to know where to look. Believe it or not, the place to go isn't outside at all. It's inside one of those very skyscrapers.

Nearly 40 species of trees, vines, and shrubs call the Ford Foundation building home. The trees and plants make up what's essentially a living lobby inside the office complex, and it's open to the public to enjoy. The building is even designed with offices spread around the atrium, so workers can enjoy the greenery, too.

Step off of busy 2nd Avenue and head into the Ford Foundation building on East 43rd Street where you'll find pathways to meander among the frilly ferns, lush shrubbery, and towering trees. The paths wind their way to a relaxing reflecting pool and fountain. Be sure to look down to admire the greenery but also gaze skyward at the incredible spectacle of a mini forest growing inside an office building. Except for chatter from fellow visitors and the bubbling of the fountain, the space is silent and serene, offering a rare escape in Manhattan.

AN UNBELEAFABLE RETREAT

WHAT: The Ford Foundation Center for Social Justice garden

WHERE: 320 E 43rd St., Midtown East, Manhattan

COST: Free to explore the gallery

PRO TIP: You'll have to show your ID before entering the garden.

Inside the Ford Foundation building, a jungle grows in the concrete jungle. Stroll through this garden when you need a break from the hustle and bustle of Manhattan.

Don't miss the sensory garden, which offers a chance to see a wide variety of plants, like bamboo, lemongrass, jasmine, and rosemary.

The garden is open anytime the Ford Foundation has an art exhibit on view, so be sure to check the organization's website for visiting hours.

UNLOCKING THE SECRETS OF MANHATTAN'S OLDEST HOME

What skeletons lurk in the closet at this historic home?

As the oldest remaining house in Manhattan, it's no surprise that this place would hold a lot of secrets and, perhaps, a few ghosts. The Morris-Jumel Mansion dates back to 1765 when it was constructed in the rural lands north of the city as a retreat for the Morris family. Given the family's British military affiliation, the Morrises didn't spend too long at the home before the city became a war zone and they fled, never to return.

HAUNTED HISTORY

WHAT: Morris-Jumel Mansion

WHERE: 65 Jumel Ter., Washington Heights, Manhattan

COST: Self-guided tours start at $10

PRO TIP: Paranormal investigation sessions tend to sell out, so book your tickets quickly.

The next occupant: General George Washington, who turned the empty house into his headquarters for about five weeks in the fall of 1776. He took advantage of the home's many windows as a strategic vantage point to watch troop movements. While Washington was headquartered here, he won the Battle of Harlem Heights, a major turning point in the war. But Washington wasn't the only military leader to use the house. Later, British troops and then Hessian troops took over the house, making the Morris-Jumel Mansion a rare example of a place that housed both sides of the American Revolution.

After the war, the newly formed United States government seized the house (because it was owned by Loyalists). Washington returned to the house in 1790 to host a luncheon with his leaders and their

Left: Located in Manhattan's Washington Heights neighborhood, the Morris-Jumel Mansion dates back to 1765. Inset: Known as Washington's War Room, this room's windows provided a strategic vantage point for George Washington to monitor troop movements.

wives, including Martha Washington, Thomas Jefferson, John Quincy Adams, John and Abigail Adams, Alexander and Eliza Hamilton, and Henry and Lucy Knox.

The house sat empty for a while until it was bought in 1810 by Stephen and Eliza Jumel, who turned the home into a showpiece. After Stephen died, US Vice President Aaron Burr courted Eliza, and she eventually married him at the Morris-Jumel Mansion, though the relationship was unhappy and brief. Eventually, the house became a museum in 1904.

Today, it regularly hosts paranormal investigations that offer a chance to ghost hunt throughout its many rooms. One more fun fact: famed playwright Lin-Manuel Miranda spent time writing *Hamilton* in Burr's bedroom at the mansion.

In addition to all of the Revolutionary War history in the house, it's important to note that the home was likely built with the labor of enslaved people. The museum points this out and explores the brutal work Black Americans would have faced there.

INTO THE WOODS

Where can you experience an old-growth forest in the city limits?

Long before concrete and pavement covered New York City, woodlands carpeted its lands. Today, one of those original forest tracts remains on the grounds of the New York Botanical Garden in the Bronx. Called the Thain Family Forest, this 50-acre woodland became a part of the New York Botanical Garden when the garden's founding director Nathaniel Lord Britton selected the land for its unique beauty and deep history. It's now considered the largest uncut expanse of New York City's original woodlands.

Visitors are welcome to stroll through the forest's paths, which were originally hunting routes for Indigenous people, and walk beneath a canopy of trees that dates back to the American Revolution. Fungi, mosses, and ferns call the forest home, along with a variety of birds, fish, and turtles. Also look out for marks on the landscape left by glaciers thousands of years ago.

The beauty of the Thain Family Forest changes with each season. In winter, snow clings onto the tree branches, giving way to snowdrop

NEW APPRECIATION FOR AN OLD-GROWTH FOREST

WHAT: Thain Family Forest at New York Botanical Garden

WHERE: 2900 Southern Blvd., Bronx

COST: $35/adult

PRO TIP: Stay on the paths in the forest and don't climb on trees or rocks.

The forest is open year-round for visitors, and it's worth visiting more than once to admire the changing seasonal splendor.

The Thain Family Forest, a 50-acre woodland, is a part of the New York Botanical Garden. Beautiful no matter the season, the forest dazzles year round.

flowers that bloom each spring. The dense canopy truly shows off in the summertime as lush leaves offer a shady respite from the hot sun before turning crispy and colorful as fall arrives.

For thousands of years, the forest has performed this seasonal dance, and researchers at the garden now work diligently to plant native species, manage invasive plants, and research the soil to keep it healthy for years to come.

LOOKING FOR LUCK

Why do performers rub a tree stump at the Apollo Theater?

Some of the biggest names in music history got their start at the Apollo Theater in Harlem. Ella Fitzgerald, Gladys Knight, Jimi Hendrix, Lauryn Hill, the Jackson Five, and Machine Gun Kelly have all graced its legendary stage for Amateur Night.

Amateur Night, the theater's signature program, runs like a talent show—except the audience is intense. Really intense. Taking the show's motto "Be good or be gone" to heart, the crowd will either cheer or boo for each performer. A chorus of boos gets the performer kicked off the stage.

Given the high-stakes drama, a little luck couldn't hurt, so before each performer starts, they rub their hand on a tree stump that sits on the side of the stage. This superstition dates back nearly a century. A tree once stood along a median a few blocks north of the Apollo, across from what was then called the Lafayette Theatre. One day in the 1920s, unemployed performers gathered around the tree hoping their singing, dancing, and comedy routines would attract the attention of the theater executives across the street. A few got hired, and the performers thought it was because the tree radiated good luck.

BE GOOD OR BE GONE

WHAT: Tree of Hope at the Apollo Theater

WHERE: 253 W 125th St., Harlem, Manhattan

COST: Tickets start around $30 for Amateur Night

PRO TIP: There's a replica of the Tree of Hope in the lobby, which you can see for free. But to see the real one, you'll need tickets to a show.

There's a colorful sculpture and a plaque at the site of the original Tree of Hope. Find it at 131st Street and Adam Clayton Powell Jr. Boulevard.

The world-famous Apollo Theater is an icon in Harlem and beyond.

When the city announced plans to fix the sidewalk and cut down the tree, everybody wanted a piece of the lucky tree. Some people collected bark, leaves, or branches. But Ralph Cooper, the creator of Amateur Night, took the stump of the tree for his show so performers could rub it with hopes the luck would transfer to them before stepping onto stage. Now called the Tree of Hope, the stump has held a place of honor on the Apollo stage ever since Amateur Night began in 1934.

Show after show, hopeful contestants hope the tree's luck will save them from boos and help propel them to stardom like so many before them.

WELL, THAT ESCALATED QUICKLY

Where can you literally step back in time?

With their click-clacks, creaks, and rumbles, the old escalators in Macy's Herald Square store sound more like a vintage roller coaster than a method of transport. But these century-old wooden escalators have stood the test of time.

On the lower floors of the gigantic 11-story shopping complex, you'll find contemporary metal escalators. Take those up and up and up and you'll notice things start getting more interesting. There, you'll see the escalators change from the modern version to the 1920s iteration. It feels like literally stepping back in time. Keep going all the way to the top floor. You'll notice some of the escalators are as wide as today's designs, while others are so narrow they can fit just one person per step. It's transfixing to watch as the wooden teeth join and separate over and over.

STEP RIGHT UP

WHAT: Wooden escalators in Macy's

WHERE: Macy's Herald Square, 151 W 34th St., Manhattan

COST: Free

PRO TIP: The store's so big that there are dining options on almost every floor.

This massive building contains 2.5 million square feet, including 1.25 million square feet of retail space, making it the largest department store in the nation and among the biggest in the world.

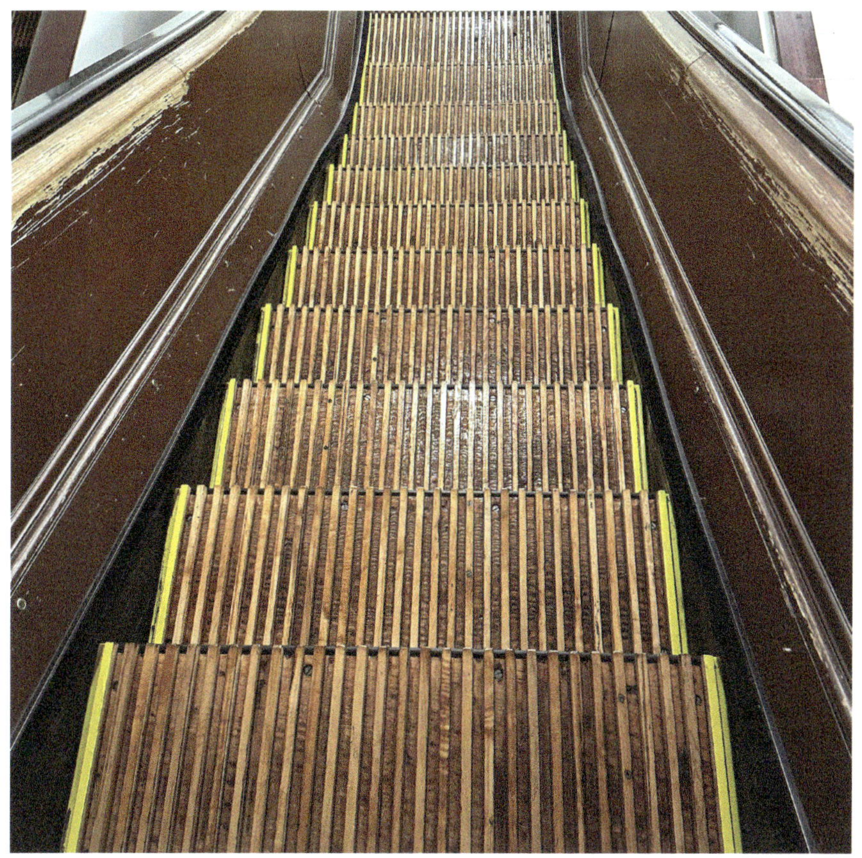

Skip the elevator at Macy's in Herald Square and use these vintage wooden escalators instead. These are some of the last wooden escalators in the world.

Though the store underwent a renovation completed in 2015, designers kept the more than 20 Otis escalators made from oak and ash woods. They're reliable and meet safety codes, store staff told the *New York Times*. Plus, they're a major attraction, given that they're some of the last wooden escalators left in the world.

Just be careful if you're wearing high heels. The treads on these escalators measure half an inch wide, meaning they're not friendly to those stilettos you may have purchased on Macy's second floor, which is home to the world's largest shoe floor featuring 280,000 pairs in 67,000 square feet.

HAUNTING THE GREAT WHITE WAY

Do ghosts really lurk on Broadway?

Theater folks are a superstitious bunch. They say "Break a leg" instead of "Good luck." They never utter the actual name of the "Scottish play." They even leave a special light called a "ghostlight" lit in the theater.

Many theaters have reported creepy occurrences, but one is known as the most haunted. That's the Belasco Theatre, opened by impresario David Belasco in 1907. Stand in front of the theater and look at the top right section of the building; you'll notice an unusual section of red brick and windows. That area was once a 10-room apartment where the peculiar Belasco lived from 1910 until he died in 1931.

THE SPIRIT OF BROADWAY

WHAT: Belasco Theatre

WHERE: 111 W 44th St., Midtown, Manhattan

COST: Free

PRO TIP: Learn even more haunted Broadway history on a tour with the fascinating Broadway Up Close; tickets cost $41/adult.

Belasco was a recognizable character. He wore the garb of a Catholic priest, even though he didn't practice religion, and he wanted to be known as the Bishop of Broadway. After his death, it seems that Belasco's spirit stuck around. Every opening night for decades, his likeness was said to be seen walking down the steps, sitting in the balcony, and then disappearing. This tradition finally stopped a few decades later with the debut of a risqué show called *Oh! Calcutta!* After that, he wasn't seen again on an opening night, but the sightings still continued on other days. Dancers have reported feeling their bottoms being pinched when no one is there, hearing a man whispering in their ears, or seeing the figure of a Catholic priest in their dressing room mirror.

Look at the top right of the photo to see where the apartment once stood.

During preservation efforts during the 1980s, staff worried that all of Belasco's heavy furniture would fall through the floor of the apartment, so they removed the church pews he used as seating. The confessional booth he used as a writing desk still stands. They decided that the apartment would never be used, instead opting to leave it empty—well, except for the ghost.

David Belasco isn't the only ghost said to haunt this theater. One of his girlfriends died after falling down an elevator shaft while leaving his apartment. She's known as the Lady in Blue, and she's also been seen numerous times, often by actors who spot her from the stage.

THE KEY TO A SECRET SPEAKEASY

Where can you see a century-old Prohibition relic?

When steel magnate Andrew Carnegie died in 1919, he bequeathed his namesake Carnegie Hall to his wife, Louise. The property included the legendary concert hall along with an adjacent building on West 57th Street and two small buildings on West 56th Street.

Little did she know, one of those buildings would soon house Club Richman, one of the most famous speakeasies in New York City. While Mrs. Carnegie was in Scotland for the summer, the property's carriage house was leased, and she was told it was for an automobile dealership. She came home in the fall of 1924 to find that it was actually being used as a nightclub. She was horrified, and she sued. *The New York Times* reported on the lawsuit with the headline "Mrs. Carnegie Sues to Oust Night Club." She described it as a "thin disguise for a public cabaret and night club," per the newspaper's report. The club's activities continued late into the night as "professional entertainers are employed and the patrons are encouraged to dance," she explained. Mrs. Carnegie thought the space was being leased as a garage, office, and apartment, not a club. The widow demanded $25,000 in damages. The club, however, kept running, becoming a popular spot during Prohibition. The late Joan Crawford even danced on its stage under her birth name, Lucille LeSueur.

The Rose Museum is packed with fascinating Carnegie Hall history, including Benny Goodman's clarinet, Billie Holiday's publicity book, and an autographed Beatles program with a misprint of Paul McCartney's name.

This complicated mechanism once was the lock for a secret speakeasy near Carnegie Hall. The Rose Museum is filled with fascinating history related to the famed concert venue.

LOCK STEP

WHAT: Speakeasy lock at Carnegie Hall's Rose Museum

WHERE: 154 W 57th St., 2nd Floor, Midtown, Manhattan

COST: Free

PRO TIP: The Rose Museum is typically open Monday through Saturday, 11 a.m. to 4:30 p.m. and before concerts.

In 1926, Prohibition officials tried to shut it down, but club leaders insisted no alcohol had ever been served there. Two years later, in 1929, the club burned down in a mysterious fire that turned its members away from the building for good.

While the club is gone, you can still see its intricate door lock in the Rose Museum at Carnegie Hall. The lock necessitated the doorman's key turning simultaneously with a member's key in two different lock chambers. According to lore, in case police showed up to raid the spot, members could use a concealed door to exit through the basement of the hall.

OH, BOTHER

What famous bear lives at the New York Public Library?

As Winnie-the-Pooh once said, "You can't stay in your corner of the forest waiting for others to come to you. You have to go to them sometimes." If you want to see Pooh Bear himself, you'll have to venture out of your corner to the corner of 5th Avenue and 41st Street. That's where the original Winnie-the-Pooh teddy bear lives, along with several of his best friends.

The stuffed animals are on display inside the New York Public Library's Schwarzman Building as part of the permanent Polonsky Exhibition of the New York Public Library's Treasures. Inside a glass display case, Pooh sits with his friends Eeyore, Piglet, Kanga, and Tigger. (Roo isn't there because that stuffed animal was lost long ago in an apple orchard). The adorable fluffy beige bear with its mohair fur, golden glass eyes, and wood shaving stuffing is more than a century old. The bear even used to growl thanks to a special mechanism.

Back in 1921, a boy named Christopher Robin Milne received a birthday gift: a teddy bear from Harrods department store in London. Named Winnie-the-Pooh, the bear soon gained several friends, and that menagerie inspired the boy's father, A. A. Milne, to write the classic Winnie-the-Pooh adventures that are still beloved today.

STUFFED WITH STORIES

WHAT: Polonsky Exhibition of the New York Public Library's Treasures

WHERE: 476 5th Ave., Midtown, Manhattan

COST: Free

PRO TIP: Expect to wait in a short line if you visit on a weekend afternoon.

Winnie-the-Pooh and his friends sit in a display case at the New York Public Library. Pooh, Eeyore, Piglet, Kanga, and Tigger delight visitors of all ages.

The toys headed across the pond to America in 1947 and remained with Milne's American publisher until they were donated to the library in 1987, a fitting home considering the library's dedication to children's literature.

You can take a piece of the storybook magic home, as the library's gift shop sells Winnie-the-Pooh tote bags, blankets, plush toys, and, of course, books.

Incredible literary treasures often rotate in and out of the Treasures exhibition, but Winnie-the-Pooh is always on display, as is Charles Dickens's writing desk.

APPLAUSE FOR THIS ARCHIVE

How can you relive some of Broadway's best moments?

There's one place in New York City where you can watch thousands of Broadway musicals without a ticket. The price of admission: free. All you'll need is a New York Public Library card.

The Theatre on Film and Tape Archive is home to more than 4,000 recordings of live Broadway, Off-Broadway, and regional theater productions dating back to 1970. You can see famed performers like Laurence Olivier in *Hamlet,* James Earl Jones in *Fences,* Angela Lansbury in *Sweeney Todd,* and Meryl Streep in *The Taming of the Shrew.* Plus, this archive at the New York Public Library for the Performing Arts includes more recent performances, such as *Fat Ham, Funny Girl,* and *Camelot.* New productions are recorded every season to live on in the archive.

Many theater professionals and students study the library of films as they prepare for their own roles as actors, dancers, set designers, costumers, and producers. But you don't have to be in show business to use this impressive archive. It's best to make an appointment in advance, though walk-ins are welcome if space allows. If you know exactly what you want to see—say, the 1976 performance of *27 Wagons Full of Cotton* featuring Meryl Streep—let the librarian

---

In addition to the theatrical performance films, the library's collection of 8 million items includes 11th-century music, 20th-century manuscripts, and contemporary hip-hop dance recordings.

At this New York Public Library branch, you can see thousands of theatrical recordings. Photo courtesy of the New York Public Library.

FROM STAGE TO SCREEN

WHAT: Theatre on Film and Tape Archive at the New York Public Library for the Performing Arts

WHERE: 40 Lincoln Center Plz., Lincoln Square, Manhattan

COST: Free with a library card

PRO TIP: Call or email in advance to set up your appointment: 212-870-1642 or toft@nypl.org.

know what you're looking for. On the other hand, if you're open to seeing anything, ask the expert staff for a recommendation. When it's time for your appointment, you'll be assigned your own station with a TV, a computer, and headphones.

One more fun fact: though it may seem like you're simply streaming a digitized film, that's not how it always works. When you request a film, a library staff member locates the physical DVD, then plays it in their control room, sending the footage to the screen before your eyes.

SERVING UP A SLICE OF AMERICAN HISTORY

Did you know that Fishs Eddy has a secret room?

The store Fishs Eddy runs by the motto "We do dishes." This beloved local shop sells plates, glasses, mugs, platters, and all manner of dishware, whether vintage or freshly designed by Fishs Eddy. The hordes of customers who pack into the store day after day are so focused on admiring the bevy of cute patterns and hilarious designs, they likely don't even notice there's a second floor above the sales showroom.

That secret second story is typically off-limits to customers, but the shop's owner, Julie Gaines, recently decided to open up her private dishware stash for limited tours. Inside, you'll find towering stacks of plates, a mug chandelier, and shelves packed with pitchers. Each salvaged item has a fascinating backstory.

There's a bowl from Tavern on the Green, a mug with a Krispy Kreme logo, and a plate with Enron's insignia. Keep an eye out for logos from Macy's, Junior's Cheesecake, Ford, NASA, 20th Century Limited, White Castle, and many more. Years ago, companies printed their emblems on dishware for marketing purposes or just to use in the office cafeteria. Other pieces feature lesser-known restaurants, like Lew Tendler's with a logo of a guy throwing a punch or classic hamburger spot The Krystal with its slogan "Take along a sack full."

THE MAIN DISH

WHAT: Fishs Eddy secret room

WHERE: 889 Broadway, Union Square, Manhattan

COST: Free

PRO TIP: Tours are typically offered on Saturdays between 2 and 4 p.m. Ask at the cashier desk.

This secret room inside the store Fishs Eddy contains a trove of vintage dishware. Plates, mugs, and saucers fill every inch of the space.

Over the decades as a collector, Gaines rescued the vintage dishware from factories, warehouses, and basements. While she sells many of the pieces she salvages—that's how the business began, after all—the antiques in her mini museum are not for sale. The oldest piece in the collection dates back to 1903. Many items in the private collection date back to the 1950s and 1960s, an era when businesses could easily order dishware with their logo from an American factory. Today, those days are gone, but the history's still alive at Fishs Eddy.

In the secret room, also look for tools that harken back to a handmade age when designers used logo books, die-cut patterns, and paint color sample tiles.

ROOSEVELT ISLAND RUINS

What's that creepy abandoned building on Roosevelt Island?

A long, skinny strip of land sits in the East River between Manhattan and Queens. These days, Roosevelt Island connects to the mainlands by bus, subway, ferry, or tram. But back in the 1800s, the island was so isolated that doctors sent smallpox patients there to quarantine. Then called Blackwell's Island, it was home to the nation's first smallpox hospital. The massive Gothic Revival building was designed in 1856 by renowned architect James Renwick Jr., who also built the Gothic chapel St. Patrick's Cathedral in Midtown.

Once a smallpox hospital, this abandoned site on Roosevelt Island has turned into ruins. Some New Yorkers want to turn the site into a public park.

As the smallpox vaccine became available, the hospital eventually turned into a nursing school, which ran until 1956. Then, the building was abandoned, leaving time to take its toll. In the years since, its roof collapsed, floor slabs disappeared, and vandals ravaged its metal details. Only a medieval-looking eerie shell of the Gothic building remains. Ivy climbs up the remaining stonework, trees sprout from inside the ruins, and metal gates cover the ground-floor windows. A fence encircles the entire site, meaning you can't actually go inside, but the castle of medical science is visible to gawk at from the street level.

A CRUMBLING CASTLE TO MEDICINE

WHAT: Smallpox hospital ruins

WHERE: Southern part of Roosevelt Island, Manhattan

COST: Free

PRO TIP: While you can get to the island via bus, subway, or ferry, the most exciting way to go is by aerial tram from Manhattan.

Some New Yorkers want to bring this secret into the light by turning the now-landmarked site into a public park, which would memorialize the victims of the COVID-19 pandemic as well as the scientists and doctors who continue to work tirelessly to help patients. Given the building's history, it's certainly a fitting location for such a tribute. For now, though, the menacing ruins on Roosevelt Island serve as a reminder of a horrific pandemic from an earlier era.

While you're on Roosevelt Island, also visit the tranquil Franklin D. Roosevelt Four Freedoms State Park, which feels worlds away from the hustle and bustle of the city.

BEST BAR DESIGN, BAR NONE

Where can you sip a drink among renowned artwork?

A storybook unfolds on the walls of Bemelmans Bar, the legendary bar inside The Carlyle hotel. If you recognize the name Ludwig Bemelmans, that's because he was the artist and writer of the beloved children's book series *Madeline,* which was first published in 1939.

Just a few years after the book's debut, The Carlyle's managing director commissioned the artist to paint large-scale wall murals depicting all four seasons in Central Park. The whimsical paintings fill the space, from the area behind the bar to the walls above its classic leather banquettes. The art features a pair of humanlike rabbits picnicking, a man gifting balloons to a child, elephants ice skating, and a man relaxing on a bench with his dog. Other sketches serve to create the ambiance of the beloved park—there's a fountain, a snack pushcart, and plenty of wispy trees. Each illustration makes for a moment of delight and offers an ample conversation starter. The paintings, which date back to 1947, comprise the only remaining Bemelmans commission open to the public.

A BRUSH WITH GREATNESS

WHAT: Bemelmans Bar paintings

WHERE: 35 E 76th St., Upper East Side, Manhattan

COST: Free to visit; cocktails start around $30

PRO TIP: There's a cover charge and a smart dress code in the evenings.

Instead of taking a salary for his painting, Bemelmans and his family received accommodations in the hotel for a year and a half.

An illustrated story unfolds on the walls of Bemelmans Bar at the Carlyle hotel. Each drawing was created by Ludwig Bemelmans, the artist and writer of the book series Madeline.

It's not just the paintings that harken back to another era. The entire experience at Bemelmans Bar feels like a lavish Art Deco escape. Waiters in white coats serve ice-cold dirty martinis on silver platters. Jazz music plays in the background. Socialites, politicians, movie stars, and moguls—all fabulously dressed—drop by for a drink.

Considering that Bemelmans is most famous for his children's books, it's only fitting that there's a kid-focused event at the venue. Each year, the hotel hosts its famous Madeline Tea inside Bemelmans Bar on select dates around the winter holiday season. Families can sing along to selections from the Madeline Song Book and enjoy a buffet meal.

A GOOD RETIREMENT PLAN

Where do playground animals go when they're past their prime?

A unique retirement community has sprung up in Flushing Meadows Corona Park. It's home to six retirees: an aardvark, a frog, a camel, an elephant, and two dolphins. Well, concrete statues of them, to be exact. Over the years, these creatures lived in playgrounds across the city and taught scores of New York City's kids, serving as a constant reminder to wait for their turn and to play nice. After countless hours of dedicated service enduring heat waves, snowstorms, many kicks from climbing kids, and a few facelifts for the greater good, they finally got a chance to retire.

Now, the retired playground animals hang out in the lush park, enjoying more restful days than in their youth. The camel, with fading layers of red and yellow paint, rests on its knees, its humps worn bare after years of serving as a seat for eager kids. Next to it, the gray elephant stretches out on its belly, its trunk rubbed raw. The other creatures gather around in the dirt, all relaxing in the shade of the surrounding evergreen trees not far from the Unisphere. Recently installed benches offer a spot for humans to sit among the animals in quiet contemplation.

While you're in Flushing Meadows Corona Park, also visit the Unisphere and the Rocket Thrower statue; both date back to the 1964 World's Fair, which was held at the park.

Though their paint is chipping and some of their features are worn, these animals still provide plenty of joy and inspiration for kids of all ages. Visitors are encouraged to offer their well wishes and take photos with the animals. Just don't climb them. As a sign at the site says: "They've had enough."

RETIRED AND LOVING IT

WHAT: Home for Retired Playground Animals

WHERE: Flushing Meadows Corona Park, Queens

COST: Free

PRO TIP: Find the animals on United Nations Avenue North, not far from Avenue of the Americas within the park.

Strong and sturdy during earlier years, this camel statue now lives in retirement at the Home for Retired Playground Animals in Queens. An aardvark, a frog, a camel, an elephant, and two dolphins also spend time as retirees.

TIME FLIES

How can you fly back to the 1960s?

Airplanes are typically known for shuttling passengers to other time zones but not other time periods altogether. Connie, however, the darling propeller plane parked at the retro TWA Hotel, whisks visitors back to the golden era of the Jet Age.

The plane, officially called a Lockheed Constellation, was revolutionary when it debuted in the late 1950s. Then the largest airliner ever built, this model could carry up to 100 people at 300 miles per hour, which was mind-blowing at the time. Constellation planes flew movie stars and President Dwight D. Eisenhower, who designated it as the model for Air Force One. Within just a few years, though, the plane went out of style when the Boeing 707 eventually sped past the abilities of Connie's propellers.

The particular Connie docked at TWA Hotel had a fascinating life. Debuted in 1958, this model flew out of John F. Kennedy International Airport (then called Idlewild Airport) as soon as the terminal opened in 1962. Later, this Connie shuttled supplies in Alaska, then became an illicit-drug-runner in South and Central America until a collector in Maine bought the aircraft. Connie sat in storage for 30 years until the developers of TWA Hotel bought the plane and painstakingly restored it back to its original glory.

Now, visitors are welcome to step onto the tarmac and climb aboard the plane, which has been transformed into a cocktail lounge. Inside, guests sip drinks while perched on plush red banquettes crowded around retro tulip tables. Some seating is even set up to look

UP, UP, AND AWAY

WHAT: Connie Cocktail Lounge at TWA Hotel

WHERE: 1 Idlewild Dr., Queens (at John F. Kennedy International Airport)

COST: Free to visit; cocktails start around $18

PRO TIP: Anyone can visit the cocktail lounge, even if you're not a hotel guest.

TWA Hotel offers a chance to travel back to the golden era of the Jet Age. This plane-turned-bar serves up themed drinks, like the Vodka Is My Co-pilot. Photos courtesy of TWA Hotel.

like Connie's original airplane seats, which are much more comfortable and stylish than the airline seats today. The cocktail menu features themed drinks, like the Vodka Is My Co-pilot and the Paper Plane. Sure, this plane can't actually take you anywhere, but with the retro vibes inside, you likely won't want to leave anyway.

It's worth staying the night at TWA Hotel or at least booking a day pass to explore all the vintage hotel has to offer, like its rooftop pool with runway views, fascinating museum exhibits, and cute photo ops.

ALL THAT GLITTERS IS NOT GOLD

What lies beneath MoMA PS1?

For any building in a cooler climate, a heating element is critical. In modern America, though, we don't likely think about our boilers or furnaces much—until they stop working on a cold day, that is. That's part of what makes Saul Melman's art piece *Central Governor* so revolutionary. It gently, deftly draws our attention to the unseen and underappreciated, turning something mundane into something beautiful.

During a six-month-long performance in 2010, Melman covered the defunct boiler at MoMA PS1 with a layer of gold leaf. The boiler, which dates back to 1902, is a hulking beast of a machine that once kept the former school building warm during wintertime. With its variety of doors, valves, and pipes, the machinery looked like a steampunk art installation even before its golden upgrade.

In some places, Melman carefully gilded every edge and every corner. In other places, he intentionally left the decoration unfinished, revealing parts of the original gray metal. In addition to his gilding, the artist also chiseled 5,000 pounds of salt block in the basement boiler room during his performance sessions. The works were intended to make allusions to the alchemical properties long associated with salt and gold. Nowadays, only the gold boiler is on view.

MoMA PS1 is a contemporary art museum affiliated with The Museum of Modern Art in Manhattan. Located inside a former school building, the museum is packed with site-specific installations as well as special exhibitions.

Artist Saul Melman turned this massive defunct boiler into a piece of modern art. The artist left parts of the boiler purposely ungilded.

BURIED TREASURE

WHAT: *Central Governor* installation at MoMA PS1

WHERE: 22–25 Jackson Ave., Long Island City, Queens

COST: Suggested $10/adult; free for New York residents

PRO TIP: During inclement weather, the exhibit may be closed, so it's best to visit on a more temperate day.

To find this golden trove, head down to the basement of the art museum and look for the sign reading "Historic Boiler Room." Be prepared to navigate a set of narrow steps and uneven bricks beneath your feet.

PERFECT PAIR

Where can you find a store that only sells one thing?

A stroll through Chinatown is always a feast for the eyes with its bustling streets, colorful decor, and sidewalk produce markets. But when it's time to dig into a feast for the stomach, one tiny shop delivers with a vast selection of chopsticks. More than 200 varieties of chopsticks fill the compact Yùnhóng Chopsticks Shop.

Neatly displayed in colorful boxes, chopsticks in a wide array of designs decorate the walls. Choose from a classic wooden set or blue-and-white-porcelain pair, each retailing for around $12. Or splurge on ornate mahogany chopsticks with intricate designs for $78 a pair. Those detailed sets feature stunning designs, like one with silver images of koi fish, sold with a carved, fish-shaped chopstick rest. Other chopsticks are made of ebony and even sterling silver. They'll make you totally rethink those prepackaged takeout chopsticks.

You'll also find chopstick accessories, such as adorable chopstick holders shaped like green leaves, beautiful butterflies, and snoozing cats. There are even chopstick cases, so you can take your utensils on the go. While the store specializes almost entirely in chopsticks, it also sells a small selection of wooden spoons and handmade silk fans.

With 50 locations in China, Yùnhóng opened its first US store in NYC's Chinatown in 2008. The Beijing-based company was even selected to provide chopsticks for the 2008 Beijing Olympics.

PICK UP A PAIR

WHAT: Yùnhóng Chopsticks Shop

WHERE: 50 Mott St., Chinatown, Manhattan

COST: Free to visit; items start at around $4

PRO TIP: This tiny shop can be easy to miss when you're strolling through Chinatown, so don't miss the address.

The compact Yùnhóng Chopsticks Shop fits a vast selection of chopsticks onto its walls. While the store focuses almost entirely on chopsticks, you can find a few spoons and silk fans.

There's a Chinese tradition that giving chopsticks brings happiness, so you might as well treat yourself and a friend to a pair.

"THIS IS A RAIDED PREMISES"

Where can you discover a piece of LGBTQ history?

Every June, people across the nation celebrate LGBTQ Pride with marches, parades, and festivals. Every one of those events has roots in New York City at The Stonewall Inn.

Back in the 1960s, the bar, which was owned by the mafia at the time, became a popular spot for gay New Yorkers. In that era, it was illegal for bars to serve alcohol to a gay person or to allow same-sex dancing. The Stonewall Inn became a safe haven where anybody "could come here and be who you wanted to be . . . and love who you wanted to love," the bar's current co-owner, Kurt Kelly, said. Police often raided bars like this, barging in to make arrests and take money from bartenders. When they did, they'd affix a sign to the door reading, "This is a raided premises."

The police tried to raid The Stonewall Inn on June 28, 1969, but the gay community fought back that night, doing kick lines like the Rockettes and throwing beer cans, eventually leading the police to barricade themselves in the bar. As the uprising continued in the area for several nights, the news spread through underground newspapers across the nation, birthing the modern LGBTQ rights liberation movement. One year later, on June 28, 1970, the first annual Pride march was held in New York City on the anniversary of the Stonewall uprising.

After the raid, The Stonewall Inn stopped operating as a bar. The building became home to a shoe store, a deli, a bakery, and an Asian restaurant. It reopened as a bar in 1987, but it wasn't known for its historical value until Kurt Kelly, Stacy Lentz, Bill Morgan and

---

In addition to the police raid sign, also check out the historic photos on the bar's walls, which document the history of the uprising.

As the sign says, The Stonewall Inn is where Pride began. Inside the bar, look for old newspaper clippings and photos documenting LGBTQ history.

Tony DeCicco bought and restored it in 2006. As Stonewall's profile rose again, a woman approached the bar and said she had the police raid sign from the Stonewall rebellion. She donated it, and now it stands in the bar's entryway, a reminder to all of the movement's history and the continued fight for LGBTQ rights.

SAVING THE STONEWALL INN'S HISTORY

WHAT: Police raid sign at The Stonewall Inn

WHERE: 53 Christopher St., Greenwich Village, Manhattan

COST: Free to visit, but buy a drink while you're there.

PRO TIP: Across the street is Stonewall National Monument at Christopher Park.

SCULPTING A VISION OF HOME

Where can you go on an artistic scavenger hunt?

Walking through the Parkchester apartment complex feels like a game of I Spy. I spy a firefighter, a child playing an accordion, a man playing a banjo, a couple of seals, and a woman and child with a cat, just to name a few. All of these figures are terra-cotta sculptures that decorate the exteriors of the red brick buildings. More than 1,000 sculptures adorn the Parkchester apartments, making it the largest sculpture garden—and perhaps the least publicized sculpture garden—in the city. The sculptures have endured for more than 80 years, though some have deteriorated recently, much to the chagrin of a group of residents who are rallying to save them.

ON A PEDESTAL

WHAT: Parkchester apartment compex sculptures

WHERE: 1589 Unionport Rd., Parkchester, Bronx

COST: Free

PRO TIP: Remember that people live here, so be respectful while looking at the artwork.

When Parkchester was built in 1940, it was the country's largest apartment complex. Metropolitan Life Insurance built the development for a population of 40,000 people, adding to it a 500,000 square foot shopping center and a central fountain. The company hired Richmond H. Shreve, whose firm had designed the Empire State Building, to draw up plans. They also hired nine artists to festoon the buildings—Gleb W. Derujinsky, Carl Schmitz, Joseph Kiselewski, Raymond Barger, Edmond Amateis, Theodore Cotillo Barbarossa, Burr Miller, Theodore Beck, and George Kratina. Each sculptor brought their signature style to the pieces, creating 100 original designs, which were then duplicated throughout the complex. While many of the pieces at eye level are

Beautiful sculptures like this one dot the buildings in the Parkchester apartment complex. There are more than 1,000 sculptures at Parkchester; see how many you can find.

colorfully glazed in red, gold, and green tones, the sculptures at the top corners of the buildings typically take on a more natural clay look.

Given the apartment complex's artistic and historical significance, the city's Landmarks Preservation Commission recommended designating Parkchester as a historic district. They made that recommendation in 1978, and advocates are still working to secure the designation, which would help protect the architecture for years to come.

Take the 6 train to the Parkchester stop, then it's just a short walk into the huge neighborhood with multiple entry points. Don't miss the Bronx Unionport Parkchester Park where you can relax next to a fountain.

A WONDERFUL WORLD INDEED

How can you pay tribute to Pops?

Despite playing on the biggest stages in music and for some of the most famous names in the world, Louis Armstrong remained humble all his life, living in a modest two-story brick home in a working-class neighborhood in Queens. Much of that is thanks to his wife, Lucille, who wanted to buy a house, even though Louis didn't think it was necessary because they'd be traveling on tour. Little did Louis know, Lucille used her own savings to buy a house in the Corona neighborhood of Queens. She envisioned it as a starter home, but once Louis saw it, he loved it and never wanted to leave.

Now, the late couple's beloved home is open for tours, offering a chance to walk through the Armstrongs' beautifully appointed living room, check out their retro kitchen, and even step inside Louis's den full of music equipment. Thanks to restoration and conservation work, the home looks exactly as it did when the Armstrongs lived here until the 1970s. Tour guides share stories about the jazz icon's musical career, offer insights into his life, and play recordings of him speaking in his instantly recognizable gravelly voice.

Across the street from the home stands a newly opened museum called the Louis Armstrong Center. It's packed with artifacts and memorabilia, like Louis Armstrong's Grammy Award

---

Louis was so beloved in the neighborhood that local kids would gather around his bus when he returned home from a trip, eager to help him carry his trumpet and suitcases inside. Lucille would fix everybody a bowl of ice cream to enjoy while they watched westerns on TV together.

for "Hello, Dolly!," a gold record for "What a Wonderful World," and a six-page love letter to his neighborhood written during the final weeks of his life. Another gem on display: a gold-plated Selmer trumpet given to him by England's King George V in 1934. The mouthpiece is engraved with "SATCHMO," a nickname Louis went by. It's presented alongside his trademark white monogrammed handkerchief, which he always wore onstage.

HITTING THE HIGH NOTES

WHAT: Louis Armstrong House Museum

WHERE: 34–56 107th St., Corona, Queens

COST: $20

PRO TIP: The museum often hosts concerts, educational workshops, and trumpet lessons. Check their website for details.

England's King George V gave this gold-plated Selmer trumpet to Louis Armstrong in 1934.

ROBOTIC RECEPTION

What would robots say if they could talk to each other?

> ## RUST IN PEACE
>
> **WHAT:** The Robotic Church
>
> **WHERE:** 111 Pioneer St., Red Hook, Brooklyn
>
> **COST:** Prices vary by event
>
> **PRO TIP:** Add your email address to the venue's mailing list at amorphicrobotworks.org/the-robotic-church to stay updated on future events.

In Chico MacMurtrie's world, robots communicate with each other through body language and sounds, from introspective solos to stirring ensemble pieces. They find rhythm through this communication, learning that working in a group makes them stronger. It's a lesson humans ought to learn, but in the meantime, MacMurtrie has dedicated decades to building machines imbued with this wisdom.

More than 50 robots live at the Robotic Church, a former Norwegian Seamen's Church (or Sjømannskirke) turned ashtray factory turned anarchist collective turned art studio. The outside of the red brick building invites intrigue with its tall, green-framed windows and curious "smo-king" sign, yet it gives no indication of what exactly is inside. And what's inside is incredible. Robots hang out on the floors and even perch on a balcony overlooking the scene. One has a body made up of chimes. Each robotic drummer is linked to an industrial-strength hand-made drum. Though the machines are capable of strumming, vibrating, and playing their own bodies to communicate, MacMurtrie is quick to point out they are not a band. Instead, he says, the robots have formed a society and communicate through their own language.

The robots' electropneumatic operating systems are made up of air coursing through tubes and wires that turn off and on—a system that seems practically human. Many of the creatures are made of metal, pneumatics, wood, rubber, and plastic, but over the last 20 years, MacMurtrie has worked on large-scale inflatables and is currently creating ceramics.

From the outside, it would be impossible to guess that a robotic community lives here. Pictures don't do justice to the incredible artistry inside The Robotic Church. Top photo courtesy of © Chico MacMurtrie / ARW, by Mathew Galindo. Bottom photo courtesy of © Chico MacMurtrie / ARW, by Robert Wright.

To create the creatures, MacMurtrie drew on his experience in live performance, art, lighting, sculpture, anatomy, and drawing. The machines are set up as a permanent installation, and the artist occasionally runs live programming at The Robotic Church. The building itself, with its dusty barnlike aroma and bare-bones design, has long made a space for voices of Brooklynites, from worshippers at the Sjømannskirke many decades ago to more futuristic residents of today.

The 50 sculptures on view were created between 1987 and 2006 and installed in the Amorphic Robot Works studio, also called The Robotic Church.

MINI CITY

Think it's impossible to see all of NYC in one day?

Gaze down at the skyscrapers of Manhattan. Step above the neighborhoods of Brooklyn. Get on eye level with a plane taking off from LaGuardia Airport. Seem impossible? At The Panorama of the City of New York, it's all possible.

The Panorama exhibit shrinks down the city of New York into a tiny model that makes human visitors feel like Godzilla. The model delighted visitors to the World's Fair in the 1960s, and it still inspires awe at its current home inside the Queens Museum. When the display debuted in 1964, it was the world's largest scale model and one of the most successful attractions at the fair, designed to welcome 1,400 visitors every hour. Back then, visitors could view the display from a balcony or aboard a "helicopter ride" around the perimeter set to narration by radio star Lowell Thomas.

This sprawling model of New York City comprises 895,000 buildings. The model debuted in 1964 as part of the World's Fair, and it still inspires awe from visitors today.

The Panorama was built by model maker Raymond Lester with guidance from well-known city planner Robert Moses (of *The Power Broker* fame). It's designed on a scale of 1:1,200. Put more simply: the model's 895,000 buildings are teeny-tiny dots atop its 9,335-square-foot canvas. In addition to iconic skyscrapers, like the Empire State Building and the Chrysler Building, you'll also see spot-on models of bridges, boats, roads, piers, and churches, in a design meant to celebrate the city's infrastructure and serve as an urban planning tool.

Updates throughout the years have added more than 60,000 new buildings, but New York City is a city that evolves constantly, meaning it's impossible to keep the model current. The model was last updated three decades ago when the city looked very different than it does now. The Twin Towers, for example, still stand on *The Panorama* today.

A walkable ramp winds around the perimeter of the display, and some parts even have glass flooring where you can peer down at the buildings beneath your feet while stepping from neighborhood to neighborhood in less than a New York minute.

VIEW FROM ABOVE

WHAT: *The Panorama* of the City of New York

WHERE: Queens Museum, New York City Building, Flushing Meadows Corona Park, Queens

COST: $8/adult suggested admission

PRO TIP: Also check out the museum's exhibit of World's Fair ephemera.

The Panorama plays a role in the 2011 movie *New Year's Eve,* during which Zac Efron's character helps Michelle Pfeiffer's character achieve her resolutions, including the dream of walking all five boroughs in one day.

A FORSAKEN FORT

What lies at the top edge of the subway map?

After the War of 1812, the United States military realized they needed to shore up defenses around the important and vulnerable island of Manhattan. If enemy troops could pass through the New York Harbor near Queens, they reckoned, it could spell disaster. Their solution? Construction of Fort Totten, located on a jutting-out thumb of land across the water from Fort Schuyler. If a ship tried to sail into the city, it would meet American forces on both sides.

Construction of the granite fortification began in 1862, amid the Civil War. It's built without rivets or bolts, meaning the stone blocks in this arched structure have been held together with the power of gravity for more than 150 years. A series of windows along the waterway offered a place for long cannons to peek through. It would take 12 strong soldiers to reload and aim a cannon to fire a 1,500-pound projectile about 2 miles. Behind the cannons, soliders darted along an open track-like area to deliver gunpowder.

Also at the fort: an elaborate chimney system where smoke could escape after cannon fire and a gunpowder room designed to cave in to extinguish any flames in case of an accident. There's one thing that's missing from the fort, though. That's its final two stories. During construction of the fort, a new type of artillery was invented, and it was so strong that Fort Totten couldn't withstand it if fired upon. How did they know? Soldiers did a test fire, which left a major hole in the fort's wall. You can still see the hole that's been there since 1864, halting construction after just two years.

A FOR EFFORT

WHAT: Fort Totten Civil War ruins

WHERE: Ordnance and Lee Roads in Fort Totten Park, Bay Terrace, Queens

COST: Free

PRO TIP: While the site is free to visit, it's best to explore on a guided tour with expert park rangers. Look for tour dates on the park's website.

Construction of Fort Totten began in 1862 amid the Civil War, though it was never completed. Today, the fascinating historic site is free to explore.

Despite its powerful design, Fort Totten never saw combat, with the exception of a mutiny when troops tried to overthrow their general during the Civil War.

Since 1864, Fort Totten has been used for casualty support, hospital care, and a wide variety of military offices. Most recently, it served as a US Army Reserve post before becoming a park.

A BAR STUFFED WITH HISTORY

Why are there wishbones hanging above this famous bar?

It's worth shuffling through the sawdust-covered floors of McSorley's Old Ale House, not just for a beer (light ale or dark ale are the only beer choices) but for some fascinating local history, too. McSorley's itself certainly isn't a secret, as the oldest continuously operated bar in the city dating back to 1854 and one of the most beloved to boot. But inside, it's packed with hidden gems that the average bar-goer isn't likely to notice.

Perhaps the most fascinating of those secrets is the two dozen dusty wishbones hanging on a lamppost over the bar. At first, it's a little jarring to see, considering their gunky appearance, but that feeling changes once you know their story. Decades ago, as "our boys" were sent off to fight in World War I, McSorley's would make them a turkey dinner before they deployed. They'd all pray and give thanks, then McSorley's would keep the wishbones as a good-luck wish for a safe return. The wishbones that remain belong to those who never came back "no matter how much we'd prayed for them to return year after year," McSorley's says.

The fragile wishbones have endured the decades hanging above the bar as a constant reminder of the soldiers' sacrifice. In 2011, a health inspector noted the layers upon layers of dust and strongly recommended that they be cleaned or moved away from the bar where dust could fall into patrons' drinks. At this point, the wishbones

---

The walls at McSorley's are covered with posters and ephemera, like an original wanted poster for John Wilkes Booth, a tribute to Harry Houdini's escape-proof handcuffs, and Babe Ruth's farewell photo from Yankee Stadium.

looked more like stalagmites with their puffy gray layers of dust. The bar's owner at the time, Matthew Maher, took the task upon himself, carefully removing each one, cleaning it, and replacing it above the bar once again. Today, they still remain in their original spot, becoming dusty once again and inviting all to remember the Doughboys of World War I.

The dusty wishbones hanging above the bar at McSorley's Old Ale House have a powerful backstory. The bar itself, dating back to 1854, is among the oldest in the city.

REMEMBERING THE DOUGHBOYS

WHAT: Wishbone chandelier at McSorley's Old Ale House

WHERE: 15 E 7th St., East Village, Manhattan

COST: Free to enter; get two beers for $8

PRO TIP: If you're not a beer drinker, the pub also sells sodas, along with a menu of sandwiches and soups.

IN CIRCULATION

How did modern medicine develop into what we know today?

Humans, it seems, have always been fascinated by learning about the bodies we inhabit. Today, that might manifest itself in searching on WebMD or being glued to a TV news segment about medical research. But long before the internet or television, giant books offered a glimpse at the inner workings of the body.

The Drs. Barry and Bobbi Coller Rare Book Reading Room is part of the library at the New York Academy of Medicine. The library houses 550,000 books and hundreds of thousands of pamphlets and images, documents how our ancestors explored the human body. In floor-to-ceiling carved wood bookcases, the reading room displays many books dating back to the 16th and 17th centuries, though some pieces in the collection date back even earlier. The library's holdings dig into the history of medicine and health, along with the field's intersection with topics like nutrition, cooking, and even botanicals. One of the strengths of the collection is in anatomy and anatomical atlases, many of which were created as collaborations between artists and physicians.

THIS LIBRARY IS TOTALLY HIP

WHAT: Drs. Barry and Bobbi Coller Rare Book Reading Room

WHERE: 1216 5th Ave., Upper East Side, Manhattan

COST: Free

PRO TIP: Tours are held at noon on the first Monday of every month (excluding holidays). No need to preregister; just meet in the lobby.

Look up at the chandeliers in the rare book room. Each one is adorned with early printers' marks, like crossed flags and a dolphin and anchor.

For example, the library is home to the famed anatomical atlas *De Humani Corporis Fabrica Libri Septem* by Andreas Vesalius, which ushered in modern anatomy when it was published in 1543. To this day, the centuries-old text is still encased in its original 16th century alum-tawed, blind-stamped pigskin cover over wooden boards, with metal clasps at the edges. The book contains extraordinary illustrations of dissections, as well as drawings of skeletons and muscular anatomy. Other books feature sketches of skeletons posed in unusual situations (like next to a rhino, for example) as well as intricate renderings of facial features.

On the first Monday of every month, the library opens its doors for a tour with an expert who will share stories about books in the collection and offer a chance to see them up close.

This extraordinary reading room on the Upper East Side is packed with rare medical books. Once a month, the library is open for tours with an expert who shares stories about the collection.

FOR THE POETICALLY INCLINED

Did you know Edgar Allan Poe lived in NYC?

Amid the highways and sprawling apartment complexes in the Fordham section of the Bronx, one building doesn't quite match. This weather-worn tiny white clapboard cottage with gray shingles and two brick chimneys sits in a small park among several busy roads. It was the final home of the famous poet Edgar Allan Poe.

Literature's favorite goth lived a nomadic lifestyle in the 1800s, but he settled in New York City with his ailing wife, Virginia, in 1846, paying $100 per year in rent for the modest home. At that time, the Bronx was a rural area, and contemporary thought suggested that Virginia could recover from her tuberculosis in the clean air of Fordham. They kept caged songbirds on the porch, and Poe would pace along the porch while gazing at the stars and thinking about his work. He also walked along the nearby Bronx River, which inspired his story "The Domain of Arnheim." During his time in the Bronx, Poe wrote some of his most famous works, including "The Cask of Amontillado," "The Bells," "Annabel Lee," and "Eureka."

Sadly, Virginia died in the home in 1847, with Poe himself dying under suspicious circumstances in 1849 in Baltimore. Poe's mother-in-law, Maria Clemm, who had lived with the couple, sold most of the furniture, but there are a few pieces in the cottage believed to be original: a rocking chair, a mirror, and the bed where Virginia died.

Today, the cottage sits in what's called Poe Park. It was moved slightly from its original location in 1913 when a road-widening project threatened to demolish the home altogether.

This humble cottage in the Bronx was once home to Edgar Allan Poe and his family. Inside the home, you can see some original pieces from Poe's lifetime.

The rest of the home is filled with period-appropriate pieces, like an antique secretary desk and a carved wooden bookshelf. Though Poe didn't write at this exact desk, he was known to write in the cottage's parlor and upstairs.

Now, the historic home also includes photographs, posters, and exhibitions exploring Poe's successful yet tumultuous life. You can explore these relics and walk in Poe's footsteps during a visit.

"QUOTH THE RAVEN"

WHAT: The Edgar Allan Poe Cottage

WHERE: 2640 Grand Concourse, Fordham, Bronx

COST: $5

PRO TIP: The cottage is open on Saturdays from 10 a.m. to 4 p.m.

RICH HISTORY IN RICHMOND TOWN

What's the history of the so-called forgotten borough?

Though it may not seem like a central destination nowadays, Richmond Town in Staten Island was once a popular stopover for travelers going between Philadelphia and New York City in the 1800s. Back then, this town in the center of Staten Island served as the bustling county seat from 1728 until government offices were moved to the town of St. George in 1898 to be closer to Manhattan.

Historic Richmond Town keeps that earlier era alive with more than two dozen buildings that explore life on Staten Island at that time. You can even step inside the buildings to walk in the footsteps of New Yorkers from years past. During the summer (May-August), explore the buildings at your own pace; during the off-season, be sure to book a tour. For a chronological experience, start inside a re-creation of a Lenape wigwam from the 1640s. Then, fast-forward to the 1700s to step inside a red clapboard home called the Voorlezer's House, which also served as a schoolhouse. A simple stone farmhouse named the Christopher House bore witness to the American Revolution and the divided loyalties of 1770s Staten Island. Inside, you'll see their no-frills kitchen and bedroom and get a sense of life for a typical family on the island. Finally, visit the 1820s-era Guyon-Lake-Tysen House, a much larger and more formal farmhouse that even New Yorkers today would dream of living in.

REWINDING HISTORY

WHAT: Historic Richmond Town

WHERE: 441 Clarke Ave., Richmond Town, Staten Island

COST: $10

PRO TIP: From May through August, costumed interpreters offer living history demos throughout the village.

Other buildings on the property include the Treasure House, which once served as the county courthouse in the late 1700s. It was named for the cache of gold coins found hidden in its walls, likely placed there by British soldiers during the Revolutionary War. Also don't miss the general store, the tin shop, and, of course, the stately Third County Courthouse building, which also serves as the visitor center.

Historic Richmond Town often hosts fun events, like Independence Day celebrations, tavern concerts, English country dances, and even a ball with vintage costumes welcomed.

Centuries ago, Richmond Town in Staten Island was a popular spot, and you can learn about its history at this historic site. This building at left, called the Voorlezer's House, served as a schoolhouse.

SANKOFA: RETURN TO THE PAST TO UNDERSTAND THE PRESENT

Why did a Union state have a history of slavery?

Some history is kept a secret because people would prefer to forget the injustices of the past. However, understanding these horrific stories is crucial to understanding the American story—and to ensuring our society doesn't commit these atrocities again in the future.

Given New York's position in the Union, many people might be surprised to find out that the city was heavily involved in the slave trade between 1625 to 1827. A marketplace located downtown auctioned enslaved people of African ancestry in the 1700s. By the mid-1700s, about one in five people living in New York City was enslaved, and almost half of Manhattan households included at least one enslaved person. For many years, those walking by the former site of the slave market would have had no idea of the history beneath their feet, but a sign now stands there at the intersection of Wall and Water Streets.

During the late 1600s through the late 1700s, about 15,000 enslaved and free Africans were buried outside the city wall at Chambers Street. The burial ground was taken over for construction as the city expanded. Centuries later, workers building an office in 1991 found skeletal remains, widely regarded as one of the most

---

Learn more about these sites and more local history on the renowned NYC Slavery & the Underground Railroad Walking Tour with Inside Out Tours (tickets cost $49/person).

The African Burial Ground National Monument includes burial mounds and an ancestral chamber decorated with the Sankofa symbol. Stand in the center of the Diaspora circle facing Africa and make a sound to hear it echo back to you.

ECHOES OF HISTORY

WHAT: Site of New York's Municipal Slave Market; African Burial Ground National Monument

WHERE: At the intersection of Wall and Water Streets; at the intersection of Duane and Elk Streets; both are in Downtown Manhattan

COST: Free

PRO TIP: Stand in the center of the Diaspora circle facing Africa and make a sound. You'll hear a strong echo as a way to make visitors feel connected to the world at large.

significant architectural finds in America during the 20th century. A preservation effort began quickly, with the site eventually becoming a national monument in 2006. A sobering memorial now stands at the site, consisting of burial mounds and a Circle of the Diaspora complete with a variety of cultural and spiritual images. Also look for an ancestral chamber decorated with the sankofa symbol, a heartlike design from West Africa that means "learn from the past to prepare for the future."

Though New York technically abolished slavery in 1827 (finally closing loopholes in 1841), the city was still implicated in slavery for many years as its economy depended on goods like sugar and cotton, both of which were produced with the labor of enslaved people.

PSSST . . . DON'T TELL YOUR SECRETS HERE

Where can you hear everybody's business?

Just outside of the iconic Grand Central Oyster Bar, there's a low-ceilinged tiled corridor that has a secret. Actually, it has a lot of secrets.

If you stand facing one of the corners and speak (or even whisper), the person in the opposite corner can hear what you're saying loud and clear, even in the bustling train terminal. Essentially, the sound carries over the arch from your lips to someone else's ears.

Spanish architect and builder Rafael Guastavino used what are now called Guastavino tiles to create the visually stunning arch in 1913. Though the builder didn't intend to create the acoustic phenomenon, he ended up designing a treat for the eyes and the ears. When Grand Central's leadership realized the auditory anomaly, they didn't advertise it. Instead, they let the news travel—quite fittingly—by word of mouth.

To this day, there's no sign marking the site inside Grand Central Terminal. But you'll likely see a crowd gathered there at any time of day, pressing their ears up to the walls to listen to sweet nothings or silly phrases from their friends. It's an especially endearing spot for a marriage proposal. Whether you choose to spill your secrets, tell a joke, or just say hello is up to you. Gossips, take note.

Grab a bite at the iconic Grand Central Oyster Bar after you spill your secrets. Not only is it architecturally beautiful like the Whispering Gallery, it's also known for its seafood and long wine list.

WHISPERED WONDER

WHAT: The Grand Central Whispering Gallery

WHERE: Grand Central Terminal lower level, 89 E 42nd St., Midtown East, Manhattan

COST: Free

PRO TIP: Make sure to speak directly into the corner of the wall for the most effective experience.

Perhaps the worst-kept secret in New York City, The Grand Central Whispering Gallery creates an auditory phenomenon. Stand in one corner and have a friend stand in the opposite corner, then speak into the corner.

PUT THAT IN YOUR PIPE AND SMOKE IT

What's on the ceiling at this steak house?

Keens Steakhouse, a New York City institution since 1885, is known for its dry-aged prime steak and its single-malt scotch collection. But astute observers know one more thing that makes this legendary spot even more special: its collection of more than 90,000 churchwarden pipes. That's the largest collection of long, narrow churchwarden pipes in the world.

Inside the old-school steak house with its wood-paneled walls, red leather barstools, and framed prints, the pipes affixed to the ceiling add to the charm. For those not paying attention, the pipes packed in their meticulous arrangement look something like a usual tin ceiling, but a closer look reveals their true story.

The tradition of checking a pipe at an inn dates back to 17th-century England. During this era, travelers kept their fragile, thin-stemmed clay pipes at their favorite inn instead of risking damage in their saddlebag. Keens began the tradition in the early 20th century, and their collection numbers more than 90,000 pipes, including some belonging to people you may recognize: Teddy Roosevelt, Babe Ruth, Will Rogers, Grace Moore, Albert Einstein, George M. Cohan, J. P. Morgan, David Belasco, Adlai Stevenson, General Douglas MacArthur, and "Buffalo Bill" Cody.

Inside the cavernous restaurant, one room is called the Lincoln Room. It's decorated with President Abraham Lincoln memorabilia, including the program the president held when he was shot by John Wilkes Booth in 1865.

Tens of thousands of churchwarden pipes decorate the ceiling at Keens Steakhouse in Manhattan. Keens maintains the largest collection of long, narrow churchwarden pipes in the world.

STEAK A CLAIM

WHAT: Keens Steakhouse

WHERE: 72 W 36th St., Midtown, Manhattan

COST: The restaurant's legendary mutton chop will cost you about $73.

PRO TIP: Be sure to make your reservation well in advance for this popular spot.

In 1885, the restaurant sat in what used to be the Herald Square Theatre District, which predated Broadway. Actors in full makeup were known to dash into the bar between acts to "fortify" themselves. By the early 1900s, Keens' Pipe Room became the spot for playwrights, publishers, producers, and journalists to gather. Though the city's theatrical home moved uptown, Keens remains as the only survivor of the early days of Manhattan theater.

PEACE OUT

What happened in this old house in Staten Island?

On September 11, 1776, not long after our nation's founders signed the Declaration of Independence, Continental Congress members agreed to an important meeting in Staten Island. There, in the cozy confines of a colonial-era house, John Adams, Edward Rutledge, and Benjamin Franklin met with Lord Richard Howe, a representative of the King of England.

In this moment amid the Revolutionary War, peace could have been possible. But during the meeting, the colonists explained that they'd only negotiate terms that included independence. The British, meanwhile, refused to allow independence. The failed meeting became the only peace conference of the war, which raged on for several more years. You can step inside the room where it happened on a tour of what's now called The Conference House. Today, the room is decorated with antique furniture and dotted with taper candles, evoking the style of the era.

The two-story stone house dates back to 1680 when King Charles II granted a generous plot of land to Captain Christopher Billopp. Billopp built a stately manor there among lush forests,

A MOMENTOUS MEETING PLACE

WHAT: The Conference House

WHERE: 7455 Hylan Blvd., Tottenville, Staten Island

COST: $5 suggested donation/person

PRO TIP: The house is located near the southernmost tip of Staten Island, so budget plenty of travel time.

Notice the large trees outside of the house? There are 13 of them, which were planted in the 1930s to represent the 13 original colonies.

This colonial-era house was the site of the only peace conference of the Revolutionary War. In this room, John Adams, Edward Rutledge, and Benjamin Franklin met with Lord Richard Howe, a representative of the King of England.

marshland, and meadows overlooking the Arthur Kill, Lower Raritan Bay, and nearby New Jersey. It became a center of hospitality in colonial times. Descendants of the Billopps lived there for many years, but eventually the house fell into disrepair and was in danger of demolition until preservationists, collectively known as the Conference House Association, stepped in during 1926 to save the building and restore it as closely as possible to its 1776 roots. Nowadays, the Conference House plays host to historic tours, plus special events like musical performances, outdoor markets, and fitness activities.

MIGHTY MEDALLIONS

Is there actually a secret at the world's most famous building?

During its construction in the early 1930s, the Empire State Building grew at a rate of four-and-a-half stories per week at its fastest. The 102-story skyscraper took just one year and 45 days of construction before it opened in 1931, breaking records not only for its height but also for its rapid assembly.

Building this feat of architecture and engineering took the dedicated efforts of about 3,400 laborers working every single day. Beautiful metal medallions in the lobby pay tribute to their work, though most visitors are more focused on getting to the top for the views than paying attention to the lobby decor. If you look closely, you'll find medallions representing many of the trade unions and craftspeople who dedicated their work to making the building into the icon it still is today. Look for 19 inlaid medallions representing workers in professions like machines, concrete, elevators, masonry, metals, electricity, heating, and decoration.

Though the medallions themselves are simple, elegant, and Art Deco—just like the building itself—each one illustrates an important story. The masonry sign, for example, remembers the workers who installed 198,328 cubic feet of limestone on the exterior of the building in just 113 working days. Another medallion recognizes the machinery laborers used to complete the building, like the Browning crane used to lay the foundation. It took 57,000 tons of steel to complete the building, and daring steelworkers were essential; the steel medallion recognizes their work. When visitors step into the elevators to be whisked 86 stories to the observatory, they're walking

---

On the way up to the observation deck, you'll get to tour a museum exhibit digging into the fascinating history of the building and the incredible workers who made it possible.

Medallions in the Empire State Building recognize the union laborers and craftspeople who made the building possible. Look for medallions representing concrete, elevators, masonry, metals, electricity, heating, and more.

in the footsteps of elevator experts whose efforts built 7 miles of elevator shafts and 68 elevators. Keep an eye out for the artwork honoring them.

Despite the Empire State Building's designation as the world's most photographed building, few know to look for these important symbols of labor history.

BUILDING AN EMPIRE

WHAT: Empire State Building labor medallions

WHERE: 20 W 34th St., Midtown South, Manhattan

COST: $44+/adult to tour the building, but free to stop in the East lobby to see the medallions

PRO TIP: Enter on the 5th Avenue side to see the medallions

CONEY CHRONICLES

What's hidden at Coney Island beyond the beaches and roller coasters?

Step right up to the Coney Island Museum, which documents the fascinating and fun history of Coney Island, known as "the People's Playground." For more than a century, New Yorkers have trekked to Coney Island each summer to relax on its sandy beaches and experience the thrill of amusement park rides. Though most visitors bolt from the subway directly to the shore or to the roller coasters, it's worth a stop at this under-the-radar museum.

Located in the shadow of Luna Park's winding coaster tracks and just a block from the beach, the Coney Island Museum's vintage ephemera evokes an earlier era of entertainment. The petite museum is packed with photos of New Yorkers on the beach, hand-painted signs, old-timey bathing suits, funhouse mirrors, soaring stilts, rare hold-to-light postcards, a carousel horse, and sculpted terra cotta sea creatures. While it's a delight to explore, the museum also does the important work of documenting and defending the honor of American pop culture, the museum's curator Lisa Mangels explains.

AN AMUSING MUSEUM

WHAT: Coney Island Museum

WHERE: 1208 Surf Ave., Coney Island, Brooklyn

COST: $5/adult (or $18 to include sideshow tickets)

PRO TIP: The museum is only open during the summer season.

It used to cost just a nickel to get to Coney Island on the subway. Today's fare will cost a few coins more, but you can still access the destination easily via public transit.

With vintage postcards and photos, the Coney Island Museum shares a historic reminder of years past. The museum is also home to old-timey bathing suits, funhouse mirrors, and even stilts. Photo courtesy of Eliza Rinn.

In earlier years, sideshows with sword swallowers, strongmen, and fire-eaters were a big part of Coney Island's culture. The tradition faded away by the 1970s, but nonprofit organization Coney Island USA revived it in a more contemporary way, and you can combine your museum ticket with a sideshow ticket.

After the museum and the show, head to The Freak Bar for a drink. Grab a seat at a vintage diner booth, play a song on the jukebox, and snap a photo in front of the Tchotchke Wall, all while sipping an ice-cold beer perfect for a hot summer day.

LAST STOP

What happened to the Old City Hall station?

Veteran New Yorkers are used to the grit and grime of the city's subways. They don't bat an eye at the gunky subway tiles, the filthy ceilings, the gum-stained floors—the list goes on. One decomissioned subway station, however, looks nothing like today's train terminals.

The Old City Hall train station, which operated from 1904 to 1945, is pristinely decorated with elegant exposed-bulb chandeliers and ornate leaded skylights. Green, tan, and cream tiles make up its vaulted ceiling beneath which trains would glide along a curved track. The subway was crowded from the outset, and leaders wanted to add more train cars and lengthen the platforms. But the updated train cars didn't quite work with the curved platform. Since the Brooklyn Bridge-City Hall station was nearby, commuters tended to walk there instead where they could catch express trains. Eventually the Old City Hall station went out of service.

Ironically, a chance to see the station nowadays is one of the most popular tickets in town. The New York Transit Museum sells tickets to tour the station, but they're harder to get than Super Bowl tickets. For a chance at tickets, you must first become a member of the museum, then keep an eye out for Old City Hall tour dates, which typically sell out in minutes. In addition to offering a chance to explore the empty station, the 90-minute tours also dig into the history of Alfred Beach's Pneumatic Tube and the development of City Hall and the subway system.

ALL ABOARD

WHAT: Old City Hall station tours

WHERE: Old City Hall Station, Downtown

COST: An individual membership costs $65, plus the tour ticket costs $50.

PRO TIP: Sign up for the transit museum's newsletter to be updated on tour sale dates.

The Old City Hall train station operated from 1904 to 1945. This beautiful station with ornate skylights and colorful tiles looks nothing like today's train stations. Photos courtesy of Marc A. Hermann, MTA New York City Transit.

Though the station is closed, there is one other way to catch a brief glimpse of it. The downtown 6 train uses the old station as a turnaround point after it terminates at Brooklyn Bridge-City Hall. If you stay on the train, you can see the old station for a few seconds while the train turns around to head uptown.

SOURCES

Art within Reach
Site visit January 21, 2024
https://www.janneysound.com/project/reach-new-york/

Encrypted Comments
Site visit January 6, 2024
Interview with Green-Wood's Vice President of Education and Public Programming Harry J. Weil, February 7, 2024
https://creativetime.org/projects/here-lie-secrets/

Remembering Langston Hughes
Site visit February 10, 2024
https://www.nypl.org/langston-hughes-atrium
https://www.nypl.org/sites/default/files/Schom-self-guide_0.pdf
https://libguides.nypl.org/Voices_of_the_Harlem_Renaissance
https://www.nypl.org/events/programs/2016/07/24/toni-morrison-%E2%80%9Cbench-road%E2%80%9D-reception

Set in Stone
Site visit February 11, 2024
https://www.nycgovparks.org/parks/VanCortlandtPark/monuments/1540
https://www.nycgovparks.org/parks/VanCortlandtPark

"Tear Down This Wall"
Site visit January 13, 2024
https://thierrynoir.com/biography/essays/berlin-wall/
https://bpca.ny.gov/place/berlin-wall-segment/
https://bpca.ny.gov/place/kowsky-plaza/

A Somber Corridor
Site visit January 13, 2024
https://www.911memorial.org/911-faqs
https://www.panynj.gov/port-authority/en/press-room/press-release-archives/2016_press_releases/port_authority_ainentranceinworldtradecentertrans.html
https://www.911memorial.org/visit/memorial/about-memorial

A Meditative Oasis
Site visit April 13, 2024
https://snug-harbor.org/botanical-garden/new-york-chinese-scholars-garden/

Talking about a Revolution
Site visit January 13, 2024
https://www.nycgovparks.org/parks/bowling-green/history
https://www.loc.gov/item/today-in-history/may-04/
https://www.history.com/this-day-in-history/new-amsterdam-becomes-new-york
https://www.nycgovparks.org/about/history/bowling-boules-bocce
https://www.nyhistory.org/blogs/horses-tail-new-york-historical-got-legendary-piece-king-george-iii-statue

Spot This Spot
Site visit January 27, 2024
https://untappedcities.com/2015/02/05/daily-what-the-false-myth-of-the-redstone-rocket-in-grand-central-terminal/
https://away.mta.info/articles/grand-central-terminal-tour-secrets-fun-facts-history/
https://johncanningco.com/blog/sky-mural-restoration-at-grand-central-terminal/
https://grandcentralterminal.com/what-to-see/
https://grandcentralterminal.com/history/#

Word on the Street
Site visit February 17, 2024
https://www.nytimes.com/1995/10/01/nyregion/neighborhood-report-jackson-heights-rewriting-the-story-of-scrabble.html

Time Travel to the 1600s
Site visit January 13, 2024

Shop Small—Literally
Site visit March 25, 2023
https://www.moonlab42.com/
https://www.timeout.com/newyork/news/peek-inside-this-teeny-tiny-58-inch-art-store-in-harlem-121222

A Sobering Sculpture
Site visits January 18 and 24, 2024
https://www.nycgovparks.org/parks/union-square-park/monuments/797
https://www.amny.com/news/history-lessons-flow-from-two-temperance-fountains/

Bewitching Art
Site visit January 19, 2024
https://www.instagram.com/p/CzAB4ODMKO-
https://www.centralpark.com/things-to-do/attractions/bethesda-terrace/
https://www.nycgovparks.org/parks/central-park/monuments/115
https://www.centralparknyc.org/locations/bethesda-fountain

True Crime in Early America
Site visit January 10, 2024
https://history.nycourts.gov/case/people-v-weeks/
https://www.independent.co.uk/news/world/americas/elma-sands-hamilton-burr-levi-weeks-b2431206.html
https://www.mentalfloss.com/article/69731/22-hamilton-lyrics-explained
https://www.allmusicals.com/lyrics/hamilton/nonstop.htm

Heart of the Ocean
Site visit January 13, 2024
https://southstreetseaportmuseum.org/about-the-titanic-memorial-lighthouse/
https://www.nycgovparks.org/parks/battery-park/highlights/12816
https://www.titanicbelfast.com/history-of-titanic/titanic-stories/a-love-story-for-the-ages
https://webarchive.nationalarchives.gov.uk/ukgwa/+/https://www.nationalarchives.gov.uk/titanic/stories/isidor-and-ida-straus.htm
https://www.nycgovparks.org/parks/straus-park/monuments/1510
https://bioguide.congress.gov/search/bio/S001000

Bug Out
Site visit February 14, 2024
https://bronxzoo.com/things-to-do/experiences/bug-carousel
https://bronxzoo.com/rainy-day-guide
https://www.timeout.com/new-york-kids/attractions/bug-carousel

Feeling Fizzy
Site visit February 16, 2024
Interview with Alex Gomberg, vice president, Brooklyn Seltzer Boys, February 16, 2024
https://brooklynseltzermuseum.org/

The Triangle Tragedy
Site visit February 25, 2024
https://www.nyu.edu/about/news-publications/news/2015/march/dennis-kroner-on-triangle-fire-anniversary.html
https://www.timeout.com/newyork/news/a-powerful-new-memorial-honors-the-victims-of-nycs-triangle-shirtwaist-fire-101123
https://rememberthetrianglefire.org/

Underground Art
Site visit January 17, 2024
https://www.timeout.com/newyork/news/youve-probably-stepped-on-this-secret-artwork-in-times-square-030923

Remembering "An Gorta Mór"
Site visits February 17, 2022, and January 13, 2024
https://www.nyctourism.com/attractions-tours/irish-hunger-memorial/
https://bpca.ny.gov/places/museums-memorials/?selected_id=264
https://media.bpca.ny.gov/wp-content/uploads/2023/05/02114000/bpca-IHM-map.jpg
https://www.irishcentral.com/culture/what-is-irish-hunger-memorial-new-york

Let Us Spray
Site visit April 26, 2022
https://www.instagram.com/graffitihalloffame_nyc
https://6tocelebrate.org/site/mural-graffiti-hall-of-fame/
https://www.atlasobscura.com/places/graffiti-hall-of-fame
https://www.tatscru.biz/project/memorial-walls/
https://www.instagram.com/tatscru/

Oh, Rats
Site visit January 27, 2024
https://timesmachine.nytimes.com/timesmachine/1955/08/10/83367742.html?pageNumber=27
https://s-media.nyc.gov/agencies/lpc/lp/2554.pdf
https://www.nytimes.com/1998/04/01/nyregion/commercial-real-estate-for-graybar-restoring-a-lost-luster.html
https://www.amny.com/news/nyc-zip-codes-1-28558957/

Pinball Wizard
Site visit January 28, 2024
https://sunshinelaundromat.com/

Any Kitsch Way
Site visit January 28, 2024
Interview with founder Dave Herman February 1, 2024
https://www.cityreliquary.org/

A Fan-tastic House
Site visit January 21, 2024
https://gothamist.com/arts-entertainment/58-joralemon-brooklyn-heights-secret-subway-exit-shaft-house-history
https://www.atlasobscura.com/places/brooklyn-townhouse-secret-subway-exit

A Mosaic Grows in Brooklyn
Site visit January 21, 2024
https://www.susangardnerart.com/

Power to the People
Site visit January 21, 2024
https://interferencearchive.org/

A Lofty Apartment
Site visit, Radio City tour January 27, 2024
https://www.msg.com/venue-rentals-event-rentals/rent-roxy-suite-radio-city-music-hall#about
https://www.rockefellercenter.com/magazine/arts-culture/radio-city-music-hall/

Peep Show
Site visit January 30, 2024
https://bedfordandbowery.com/2019/08/cinema-secret-at-ifc-peepholes-let-passersby-watch-movies-in-miniature/

Unlocking a Mystery
Site visit January 30, 2024
Interview with Phil Mortillaro, July 23, 2024
https://streeteasy.com/blog/greenwich-locksmiths-smallest-manhattan-building-wont-leave-village/
https://www.instagram.com/reel/C0ezjcOOWKQ/
https://www.greenwichlocksmiths.com/aboutgreenwich/

A Hidden Holocaust Memorial
Site visit January 27, 2024
https://www.nycourts.gov/courts/AD1/centennial/memorial.shtml
https://www.nytimes.com/1988/07/27/nyregion/a-memorial-to-holocaust-is-approved.html
https://www.ajc.org/news/ajc-survey-on-holocaust-knowledge-among-americans
https://www.nbcnews.com/news/world/survey-finds-shocking-lack-holocaust-knowledge-among-millennials-gen-z-n1240031
https://www.nyc.gov/site/dclapercentforart/projects/projects-detail.page?recordID=90
https://www.nycgovparks.org/parks/riverside-park/highlights/14356
https://ephemeralnewyork.wordpress.com/2014/08/18/a-riverside-park-holocaust-memorial-never-built/
https://flatironnomad.nyc/history/memorial-to-victims-of-the-injustice-of-the-holocaust/

Eat like a Founding Father
Site visit January 13, 2024
https://www.fraucestavernmuseum.org/the-long-room-exhibition
https://www.fraucestavernmuseum.org/evacuation-day-101
https://fraucestavern.com/new-york-fidi-battery-park-downtown-lower-east-side-tribeca-city-hall-south-street-seaport-fraunces-tavern-about
https://www.hmdb.org/m.asp?m=20237

A Weird Wax-travaganza
Site visit January 21, 2024
https://theodditiesfleamarket.com/house-of-wax
https://www.scribd.com/document/328862506/House-of-Wax-Menu
https://www.nytimes.com/2016/10/24/nyregion/brooklyn-bar-house-of-wax-alamo-drafthouse.html

Heart of Stone Street
Site visit January 13, 2024
https://www.timeout.com/newyork/news/theres-exciting-new-energy-on-the-oldest-paved-street-in-nyc-092523
https://www.stonestreetnyc.com/history

A Marilyn Moment
Site visit January 27, 2024
https://www.nytimes.com/2017/01/13/nyregion/marilyn-monroe-skirt-blowing-new-york-film.html
https://www.nytimes.com/2011/01/07/nyregion/07monroe.html
https://www.youtube.com/watch?v=g_1Pe1gWxnc
https://www.youtube.com/watch?v=fIh6HDeXKGY
https://www.youtube.com/watch?v=70GcyLYcLsM
https://web.archive.org/web/20240416233724/
https://onthesetofnewyork.com/thesevenyearitch.html
https://onthesetofnewyork.com/thesevenyearitch.html
https://www.reuters.com/article/idUSTRE75I2NM/

"Ain't Afraid of No Ghosts"
Site visit January 30, 2024
https://www.nyctourism.com/attractions-tours/hook-ladder-company-8-tribeca/
https://roadtrippers.com/magazine/hook-and-ladder-company-8-ghostbusters/

An Extremely Hip History
Site visit February 17, 2024
https://www.timeout.com/newyork/news/celebrate-hip-hop-history-month-with-this-exhibit-in-the-bronx-110322
https://www.atlasobscura.com/places/kool-hercs-block
https://workforcehousinggroup.com/1520-sedgwick-avenue-bronx-ny/

The Tale of the Moving Statue
Site visit January 27, 2024
https://www.nycgovparks.org/parks/central-park/highlights/11248
https://www.nyrr.org/about/history
https://www.nyrr.org/about/hall-of-fame/fred-lebow
https://www.timeout.com/newyork/news/trace-the-nyc-marathons-racial-justice-roots-in-this-new-new-york-historical-society-exhibit-102423
https://abc7ny.com/tcs-nyc-marathon-fred-lebow-statue-central-park/5662399/

Pipe Dreams
Site visit and Tour at NBC Studios, January 4, 2024
https://www.youtube.com/watch?v=IPn8UHcmC7U
https://www.thetouratnbcstudios.com/

A Masterpiece for the Original Muckraker
Site visit June 19, 2022
https://www.thegirlpuzzle.com/concept
https://www.governor.ny.gov/news/governor-hochul-announces-opening-girl-puzzle-monument-honoring-nellie-bly
https://blogs.loc.gov/headlinesandheroes/2022/11/nellie-bly-blackwells-island/

https://www.heinzhistorycenter.org/learn/women-forging-the-way/nellie-bly-around-the-world/

A Legacy of Self-Determination and Freedom
Site visit and tour February 20, 2024
https://weeksvillesociety.org/visit/tours/
https://weeksvillesociety.org/about-us/

An Ink-spired Adventure
Site visit May 7, 2023
https://southstreetseaportmuseum.org/bowne-co-stationers/
https://southstreetseaportmuseum.org/fresh-prints/

Check Out This Checkmate
Site visit January 27, 2024
https://vault.si.com/vault/1982/08/30/chess-reaches-new-heights-with-a-four-story-board-in-new-york-city
https://www.nytimes.com/2012/03/25/nyregion/melvyn-kaufman-developer-who-shaped-manhattans-streetscape-dies-at-87.html

Buried History
Site visit January 27, 2024
https://www.centralparknyc.org/locations/seneca-village-site
https://www.centralparknyc.org/articles/seneca-village
https://www.centralparknyc.org/activities/guides/discover-seneca-village
https://s3.amazonaws.com/assets.centralparknyc.org/media/documents/SenecaVillage_DownloadableMap_2024.pdf

Coke That Causes a Stir
Site visit February 6, 2024
https://www.lexingtoncandyshop.com/

For the Birds
Site visit January 6, 2024
Interview with Green-Wood's Sara Evans February 9, 2024
Interview with researcher Eric Thompson March 4, 2024

Deep Roots
Site visit February 17, 2024
https://www.nycgovparks.org/parks/alley-pond-park/highlights/19645

A Trip down Memory Lane
Site visit February 17, 2024
Interviews with Dan Treiber and Reina Mia Brill February 17, 2024
https://www.dansparentshouse.com/pages/about

A Bright Idea
Site visit February 11, 2024
https://www.nycgovparks.org/parks/fort-washington-park/highlights/11044
https://historichousetrust.org/houses/little-red-lighthouse/

An Arch-itectural Marvel
Site visit February 11, 2024
https://www.nytimes.com/1988/06/05/realestate/streetscapes-seaman-drake-arch-encrusted-relic-mid-19th-century-inwood-estate.html
https://www.dnainfo.com/new-york/20091014/manhattan/19th-century-marble-arch-for-rent-inwood-needs-little-tlc/#

A Growing Secret in Midtown
Site visit February 15, 2024
https://www.fordfoundation.org/about/the-ford-foundation-center-for-social-justice/visitor-informat
ion/

Unlocking the Secrets of Manhattan's Oldest Home
Site visit February 11, 2024
https://morrisjumel.org/

Into the Woods
Site visit February 14, 2024
https://www.nybg.org/garden/forest/
https://www.nybg.org/garden/forest/natural-history-of-the-forest/

Looking for Luck
Site visit and interview with Billy "Mr. Apollo" Mitchell, historian and ambassador at the Apollo Theater, February 21, 2024
https://www.apollotheater.org/history

Well, That Escalated Quickly
Site visit January 13, 2024
https://www.nytimes.com/2015/11/26/nyregion/macys-historic-wooden-escalators-survive-renovation.html
https://www.forbes.com/sites/michaellisicky/2021/04/10/does-macys-need-to-be-the-worlds-largest-store/?sh=3d19c3663283
https://34thstreet.org/activities/macys-herald-square

Haunting the Great White Way
Site visit February 24, 2024
Broadway Up Close Tour—The Ghostlight Tour: Haunted Broadway
https://shubert.nyc/theatres/belasco/

The Key to a Secret Speakeasy
Site visit March 2, 2024
https://timesmachine.nytimes.com/timesmachine/1924/11/27/issue.html
https://www.nytimes.com/1929/09/23/archives/night-fire-wrecks-the-club-richman-forger-stable-of-carnegie-horses.html
Carnegie Hall Public Relations Staff

Oh, Bother
Site visit February 29, 2024
https://www.nypl.org/blog/2022/08/21/happy-birthday-winnie-pooh

Applause for This Archive
Site visit and interview with Patrick Hoffman, director, Theatre on Film and Tape Archive at the New York Public Library for the Performing Arts, March 4, 2024
https://www.nypl.org/locations/lpa/theatre-film-and-tape-archive

Serving Up a Slice of American History
Site visit and interview with Izzy Benner and Fishs Eddy staff, March 2, 2024

Roosevelt Island Ruins
Site visit June 19, 2022
https://rioc.ny.gov/178/Smallpox-Hospital
https://www.theruin.org/

Best Bar Design, Bar None
Site visit February 23, 2024
https://www.rosewoodhotels.com/en/the-carlyle-new-york/dining/bemelmans-bar
https://www.rosewoodhotels.com/en/the-carlyle-new-york/media/press-kit/history-of-bemelmans

A Good Retirement Plan
Site visit February 21, 2024
https://www.nycgovparks.org/news/press-releases?id=22102
https://www.nycgovparks.org/parks/flushing-meadows-corona-park/history

Time Flies
Site visit February 17, 2024
https://www.twahotel.com/connie-airplane/cocktail-lounge
https://www.twahotel.com/connie-airplane/connies-history
https://www.twahotel.com/connies-restoration

All That Glitters Is Not Gold
Site visit February 23, 2024
https://www.instagram.com/reel/C0hTSThR7M9/?utm_source=ig_web_copy_link
https://www.momaps1.org/programs/85-artist-interventions

Perfect Pair
Site visit February 25, 2024
https://www.timeout.com/newyork/shopping/yunhong-chopsticks-shop
https://www.explorechinatown.com/Images/photomosaic/gallery1.html

"This Is a Raided Premises"
Site visit and interview with Kurt Kelly, March 5, 2024
https://guides.loc.gov/lgbtq-studies/stonewall-era
https://parks.ny.gov/historic-sites/stonewallinn/details.aspx

Sculpting a Vision of Home
Site visit February 17, 2024
https://www.facebook.com/theparkchesterproject/posts/3047424078904478/

https://6tocelebrate.org/neighborhood-items/parkchester-the-bronx
https://www.nytimes.com/2022/05/20/realestate/streetscapes-parkchester-bronx.html
https://pix11.com/news/local-news/bronx/bronx-woman-on-mission-to-protect-hundreds-of-terracotta-sculptures-in-parkchester/
https://www.facebook.com/theparkchesterproject/about
https://www.instagram.com/theparkchesterproject/
https://www.instagram.com/p/CkImrnru7sA/ https://www.instagram.com/p/Cfoi-qGOct4/ https://www.parkchesternyc.com/about-us/history/

A Wonderful World Indeed
Site visit and tour February 17, 2024
https://www.louisarmstronghouse.org/faq/

Robotic Reception
Site visit and tour with Chico MacMurtrie February 24, 2024
https://www.brownstoner.com/history/past-and-present-the-norwegian-seamans-church/
https://amorphicrobotworks.org/the-robotic-church

Mini City
Site visit February 21, 2024
https://queensmuseum.org/exhibition/panorama-of-the-city-of-new-york/

A Forsaken Fort
Site visit and tour March 2, 2024
https://www.nycgovparks.org/parks/fort-totten-park
https://www.nycgovparks.org/parks/fort-totten-park/highlights/12150

A Bar Stuffed with History
Site visit February 28, 2024
https://www.nytimes.com/2011/04/07/nyregion/07wishbone.html
https://mcsorleysoldalehouse.nyc/a-tour-of-mcsorleys/
https://mcsorleysoldalehouse.nyc/matty-maher-an-institution-at-an-institution-mcsorleys-dies-at-80/
https://www.facebook.com/McSorleysOldAleHouse1854

In Circulation
Site visit and tour with Arlene Shaner March 4, 2024
https://www.nyam.org/library/connect/visit-library/

For the Poetically Inclined
Site visit and tour with Roger McCormack February 10, 2024
https://bronxhistoricalsociety.org/poe-cottage#visit

Rich History in Richmond Town
Site visit and tour March 1, 2024
https://www.historicrichmondtown.org/visit
https://www.historicrichmondtown.org/historic-houses/2018/7/26/voorlezer
https://www.historicrichmondtown.org/events
https://www.nycgovparks.org/parks/latourette-park-and-golf-course/highlights/12139

Sankofa: Return to the Past to Understand the Present
Site visit February 24, 2024
NYC Slavery & the Underground Railroad Walking Tour February 24, 2024

Pssst . . . Don't Tell Your Secrets Here
Site visit and Grand Central tour November 27, 2023
https://grandcentralterminal.com/what-to-see/
https://www.oysterbarny.com/about/
https://www.history.com/news/grand-central-terminal-secrets-myths

Put That in Your Pipe and Smoke It
Site visit April 22, 2024
https://www.keens.com/historyofkeens/
https://www.keens.com/privateevents/
https://www.facebook.com/KeensSteakhouse
https://www.instagram.com/p/BLeqJZ3BDrV/

Peace Out
Site visit April 13, 2024
https://conferencehouse.org/
https://www.history.com/topics/american-revolution/american-revolution-history

Mighty Medallions
Site visit April 3, 2024
https://www.esbnyc.com/about
https://www.esbnyc.com/about/history
https://www.facebook.com/profile/100044314093645/search/?q=medallion
https://www.history.com/news/10-surprising-facts-about-the-empire-state-building

Coney Chronicles
Interview with Lisa Mangels, Curator of Coney Island Museum April 25, 2024
https://www.coneyislandmuseum.org/
https://www.instagram.com/coneyislandmuseum/
https://www.pbs.org/wgbh/americanexperience/features/coney-timeline/ https://www.facebook.com/coneyislandmuseum/photos/pb.100063660785386.-20000/5120984227970786/?type=3

Last Stop
https://nypost.com/2023/10/20/old-city-hall-subway-station-is-nycs-hottest-ticket/
https://www.nytransitmuseum.org/oldcityhall/

INDEX

Creepy crawlers aren't so creepy when they're on this playful carousel in the Bronx.

Think it's impossible to see all of New York City in one day? Think again.